SECRET THOUGHTS
of an
ADOPTIVE
MOTHER

SECRET
THOUGHTS
of an
ADOPTIVE
MOTHER

Jana Wolff

Andrews and McMeel
A Universal Press Syndicate Company
Kansas City

Library of Congress Cataloging-in-Publication Data

Wolff, Jana.
    Secret thoughts of an adoptive mother / by Jana Wolff.
      p. cm.
    ISBN 0-8362-2186-9 (hardcover)
    1. Interracial adoption—United States—Case studies.
    2. Open adoption—United States—Case studies.
    3. Adoption—United States—Case studies.
      I. Title.
HV875.64.W65   1997
362.7'34—dc20   96-26394
                                                      CIP

Book design by Top Dog Design

ATTENTION: SCHOOLS AND BUSINESSES

Andrews and McMeel books are available at quantity discounts with bulk purchase for educational, business, or sales promotional use. For information, please write to: Special Sales Department, Andrews and McMeel, 4520 Main Street, Kansas City, Missouri 64111.

*D*edicated with love
to my son's mother
and mine.

CONTENTS

ACKNOWLEDGMENTS

I am so lucky. I have too many people to thank. These are some of them:

Dick Adler married my mom when I was seventeen. He taught me that being my father was something more than biological happenstance. With Ree Adler as my mother, biology turns out to be a very good thing. They have been great parents to me.

I have a crush on the man that I married. Howard Wolff is an extraordinary person, a perfect partner, and modest enough to accuse me of hyperbole.

My heart has gotten a lot of exercise since Ari Wolff came into my life. He is an inadvertent teacher, a natural amphetamine, an irresistible love.

Some of the values that shape and distinguish our family today are ones which were passed on by Sylvia and Bill Wolff. We've been nourished along the way by very special friends like Edith and Max Taylor and Tinker and Bob Whitaker, all four of whom I'd like to be when I grow up.

If you could pick your relatives, I would have picked the siblings I got: Kathy, Linda, Pattie, and Tom. And I can say the same of my siblings-in-law—Aviva, Dvora, and Ronit—who were, luckily, part of the package deal. Gertrude "Nana G" Ruddy is not related but feels that way.

I've got great friends who are more sure of me than I am sometimes. Especially Elliot Sobel and Perry Goldstein, proprietors of intimacies based on twenty-three years of friendship. And Leslie Brower, whom it seems I've always known. Nancy Hanson is the kind of friend who will write my deadlines in her calendar and call me to see if I've met them.

Thankfully, there are three professionals who worked on my behalf and knew what they were doing. Hillel Black is the one who found me in a crowd at the Maui Writers Conference. Wendy Lipkind was soulful as my first reader and skillful as my agent. Editor Dorothy O'Brien used her pencil with precision and kindness and escorted me to this place.

Sharon Kaplan Roszia, who knows so much about adoption, treated me as if I knew as much and encouraged me to find out more.

Deserving final thanks are those women with enough courage to let their children fall in love with other mothers. They are heroes, in a way.

PROLOGUE

B.C.: Before Child

My mother tells me that, as a little girl, I used to give birth to my doll Kate several times a day as I let her fall out from under my T-shirt. Careful to support the baby's head, I'd pick her up and stick a little plastic bottle filled with pretend juice or milk to her lips. I was a very good mother.

Thirty-something years later, I realize that delivering Kate was the closest I ever got to giving birth. Many little girls play "mommy" just like I did, but none of us dreams of becoming an adoptive mother. Adoption is not in the repertoire of child's play. It is nothing to which children aspire and a process for which we, as adults, are woefully unprepared.

As I went through the adoption process (ready, at any moment, to pull out if there was an easier way), I knew that I was on uncharted ground emotionally, with no road map and no role models. I could follow the how-to books and generous advice offered to get me from Step A to Step B (from adoption application to baby), but how was I supposed to be *feeling* while jumping through those hoops? I had heard about emotions that fell cleanly under the headings of "happy" and "sad," but my feelings—of amusement and terror, of surrealism and sarcasm, of familiarity and alienation—didn't quite fit. I had no way of knowing if I was weirder than my application let on, by virtue of the very strange feelings I was having throughout the adoption process.

An *open* adoption such as ours is one of the most amazing experiences of all time: amazingly funny, amazingly threatening, amazingly touching. A complete stranger becomes a lifelong relative and allows her child to become yours. An *interracial* adoption such as ours is one of the biggest experiences of a lifetime; in it, you'll find big hearts, big heartaches, big lessons. You do not resemble your child in the slightest way, and you can't possibly know the things that you are responsible for teaching him or her. Open adoption and interracial adoption have this in common: They both evoke the truth; there's no hiding behind either.

With the dissolving secrecy of adoption, feelings that were once taboo are less so. As I leaked a few of my secrets—first to dear friends and then to total strangers—I realized that other adoptive mothers also have resented their long-awaited children at times, not to mention their useless monthly periods. They can't seem to resolve the anger/appreciation equation toward their children's birth mothers, either; nor can they ever really understand the desperate capability of a woman to give birth and let go.

The process of adopting a child pushes your personal envelope as a woman, as a mother, and ultimately, as a human being. It takes more courage than you think you have, offers more self-knowledge than you think you want, and reassembles your characteristics into someone familiar but changed. It took me a lot longer to become a mother than it did to adopt a baby. This is a true story about doing both. It is my hope that, by sharing my story, yours will be even better.

To Produce
or to Purchase?

Either way, it's gonna cost.

*B*arren. It's a word that sounds barren.

My self-image was filled with nasty adjectives, but *barren* was not one of them. With the exception of my unfortunate cowlicks, moody self-esteem, and tendency to blow a joke's punch line, I thought of myself as fairly well adjusted and very healthy—filled with energy, nearly vegetarian, passionately in love—the most unbarren person around. Would a barren woman take step-aerobics classes Tuesdays, Thursdays, and sometimes Saturdays? Would she get picked as shortstop for a coed softball team? Would she regularly choose rice pilaf over fries? Would she sneak in a long lunch with her *husband* on a weekday? I don't think so.

At thirty-six, I was too happy to be barren. The only thing I was incapable of conceiving was the fact that I was incapable of conceiving. It never occurred to me that I could be healthy, active, successful, happy, *and* infertile.

In spite of my vitality, the reproductive eggs I took for granted for three and a half decades were now middle-aged. "Twenty-year-old bodies were made to conceive babies," clucked a fifty-something nurse to me one day at the obstetrician's office. Feeling developmentally delayed and somewhat defensive, I wanted to justify my reasons for taking so long to find the right partner and for spending a few carefree years together as newlyweds before tossing the diaphragm we had been so good about using.

My husband and I had talked about whether we would *want* kids, not whether we could have them. We talked about "when" with the presumptuousness of two people planning a vacation. We were delusional enough to believe the choice was ours. Three years into our marriage, we decided it was time for a family. I figured we might get pregnant that first unprotected month and determined that it was inevitable by the third. Eighteen months later, after his-and-her tests revealed no apparent medical reasons why we couldn't conceive, we made an appointment at the Pacific In Vitro Fertilization Clinic.

I remember one January morning at seven A.M.; my husband and I had driven in separate cars through rush-hour traffic to the hospital where the clinic was located. On the way, I ate a bagel, put on lipstick, and wondered how many other commuters were about to make a baby. At the ninth-floor clinic desk, we were given a plastic cup and directions to room 911, just next to the elevator. There, in our cozy cubicle, under buzzing white fluorescent lights, we had to perform: We didn't make love, we just made sperm. I had to leave for an eight o'clock meeting.

How those sperm—after being fortified in the baby lab and later inserted directly into my waiting cervix—could miss is incomprehensible to me. But they did. Four times in four months.

The promise of pregnancy taunted us every month for years. Basal temperature charts, LH surges, laparoscopy, Clomid, hCG injections, sperm washing, insemination, asexual sex, and many other steps along the continuum. . . . We were victims of fertility humility.

They never did find out why we couldn't conceive. Couldn't point to endometriosis or blame it on my scar tissue; couldn't fault my husband's sperm count or testicle temperature. Without a concrete physiological reason for our infertility, I was quick to fill in with emotional explanations: maybe we didn't want a baby enough; maybe we weren't meant to be parents; maybe we were being punished for all that premarital sex.

We had long since lost our senses of humor about this, and were losing hope each month I got my period. I was getting weepy; we were getting boring. We kept putting our lives on hold—no, we can't plan a bike trip to the Rockies this summer; no, I shouldn't change jobs right now; let's keep this clunker car; let's not—until we didn't have much of a life left to hold. With dwindling balances in our economic and emotional accounts, we were faced with a choice: keep fighting our bodies or start looking into adoption. Produce or purchase? Our OB's advice: "Take a break. You'd be amazed at how many women get pregnant when they stop trying so hard."

That rubbed me the wrong way. I never bought into "The Theory of the Type-A Uterus": If you would only relax, you'd get pregnant. Why was it, then, that thousands of stressed-out, drugged-out, strung-out women had kids?

In spite of our obstetrician, we decided to stop trying to make our bodies do what they didn't seem to want to do. We were not so much running toward adoption as running away from the conception roller coaster. We stopped far short of where technology could lure us, but had gone far enough to feel deflated: tired, sad, and looking for someone or something to blame.

With exasperation as our fuel, we quit being fertility junkies and started looking into adoption. Sex became less of a homework assignment once we stopped trying to procreate. Slowly, we remembered how fun it used to be.

COULD WE LOVE SOMEBODY ELSE'S CHILD?

What if we get a dud?

I started looking closely at kids. The sayings and songs about the beauty of children can only be metaphorical. Frankly, I saw a lot of dogs. On one errand-rich Saturday morning, while standing in line at the post office, dry cleaners, and then grocery store, I saw runny noses, blotchy red scalps, old-man faces. . . . Couldn't their mothers see the same? On average, I'd admit that kids look cuter than grown-ups, but that's not saying much.

Baby food and life insurance commercials wax poetic about the angelic innocence of youth, the inner beauty of every child. But I find it hard to tune into inner beauty when a kid is screaming or drooling or calling another angel a "doo-doo head." I must be missing something.

It's hard enough to imagine loving somebody else's child. What if the baby we adopt turns out to be a dud? No personality. Not cute. None of our endearing features or charming characteristics; no aptitude for our skills or talents.

We used to joke about the poor kid who might inherit the worst of our combined features: big nose, freckles, a long second toe, constipation. The child we really dreamed of was always a girl—she'd have green eyes, light olive skin, thick black hair, along with a winning personality and intellect to boot.

What if she turned out to be a he? A he with thick glasses, pumpkin-colored hair, and a wimpy attitude? Granted, maybe we could influence his attitude, even his quirks, but his looks would have nothing to do with ours.

Adoption often unites families that don't match. I've seen their smiling photos in adoption ads: One sister with straight, black hair holds the hand of another who looks like Goldilocks; a dad rubs his Roman nose against his daughter's small, flat version; a grandma's narrow face caresses her grandson's wide one; and a brother's short, stumpy legs skip alongside his sister's long, lean limbs. It's their captions, not their looks, that inform me they are families.

How important are looks? The grown-up in me says,

"Appearance isn't everything, beauty is only skin deep, you can learn to love somebody's looks." But it's tough to sustain mature behavior under stress. Meeting your adoptive baby is like being set up on a blind date with someone you will have to spend the next eighteen years with. You care about looks, because you desperately want to fall in love with the stranger who will be your child.

THE HOME STUDY: MR. & MRS. PERFECT

Your house will never (and need never) be this clean again.

You house is unnaturally clean. Not only did you vacuum, dust, and then scrub the toilet bowl in the guest bathroom, you bought flowers for the living-room coffee table (not an arrangement, just a casual looking bunch), you framed your wedding photo (finally), and you put your niece's drawing of a rainbow up on the fridge with two balloon magnets. Does this look like the perfect home for a baby or what?

You carefully picked your clothes and practiced answers to questions like: "How would you discipline your child?" and "How would you tell your child about adoption?" and "How does the rest of your family feel about this?" Then the doorbell rings.

This mandatory preplacement hoop to jump through—the home study—is carried out by a licensed social worker in your home. For somewhere around $1,000, you spend about ninety minutes showing your assigned M.S.W. around your spiffy place and try to answer questions about your upbringing, your family, your relationships, your ideas on child rearing, your reasons for wanting to adopt, your child-care plan, your infertility. All the while, your visitor is taking notes or tape recording for the purpose of writing a report that gets sent to an adoption agency, or a court, or a lawyer, or all of the above. (After all, it *is* everybody's business that your sperm count is low.)

You want her to think you are the greatest couple alive, to stop the interview and exclaim: "You are much too wonderful to spend another childless night. Let me run out to the car and get you the most beautiful and healthy newborn baby there ever was. And by the way, she's got your eyes!"

Ms. Social Worker doesn't really have any babies to taunt you with; she doesn't even need to fall in love with you; she just needs to report that you are "fit" to be parents, which she almost always does.

We received a copy of our report about a month after the visit. The very last sentence of the nine-page treatise held our sought-after stamp of approval: "Based on the aforementioned, the evaluation criteria have been successfully met." Translation: You're neither a criminal nor a child abuser; your marriage and your house are not in shambles. True cause for celebration.

After going through the home study process—one of many humbling steps along the grovel train—you may resent the power that your social worker and others have over you. "Some of these gatekeepers couldn't even pass their own tests," you might catch yourself thinking. You're also likely to resent the fact that "normal" people (like most every one of your friends) haven't had to pass a friggin' exam to have a baby. We've got a neighbor who screams at her son for talking loudly . . . *she's* the one who should have had to pass a test. I've thought the same thing about people who smack their kids, ignore them, or quiet them with candy.

Little did we know that the real tests were ahead of us, not behind us. It felt like we had come so far already. We had read all the books cheerleading wanna-be parents through the adoption process; we had talked to doctors and counselors and friends of friends. We had hung on the words of wise strangers who had adopted from places as different as Bucharest and Buffalo. We had heard horror stories and happy stories, but remembered the first kind more vividly. We had signed up with two adoption agencies. One was shut down by the feds soon after absconding with our deposit and lots of other baby down payments. The other was completely legitimate; we figured our names might get to the top of their list by the time we reached sixty. Fortuitously, someone gave us the name of a young lawyer in L.A., just going off on her own as an adoption specialist. After a phone conversation, we decided that we could afford her and we could understand her. Things were looking up.

Upon signing on with an adoption attorney, we were asked for two things: $1,500 and a picture book illustrating our lives and describing our hopes. We sent the book first, but we held out for one more menstrual cycle before letting go of the money . . . just in case.

It took us weeks to put together that book. We dug through old photographs in search of pictures that made us look good. With a baseball hat on, you could barely see my husband's thinning hair, and soft lighting was better than Retin-A for the wrinkles around my eyes. Luckily, we live in Hawaii, where sunsets and palm trees aren't too far-fetched as backdrops. Photographs that showed us playing with nieces and nephews rose to the top of the pile. We felt like idiots posing in front of our townhouse, while a passing neighbor said "Cheese," and mildly hypocritical about borrowing a hammock to make the backyard look like it was occasionally used.

The hardest part, though, was to genuflect in writing and come up with the notorious "Dear Birth Mother" letter.

Here is what I wanted to write:

Dear Birth Mother:

Screw you. Do you think I want to beg a complete stranger for a kid whose own mother doesn't want him? You messed up and now you get to sit in judgment of the perfect parents for your baby. . . . What do you know about parenting? About perfection? How will you choose, anyway? Will it be the prettiest couple? The richest? The hippest? The most devout? We wouldn't win on any of those counts.

If, by some fluke, you do us the great honor of pronouncing us fit to be adoptive parents, what will we owe you? Will we have to support you for the rest of your life? Name the kid after you? And what will happen once you realize what you've done? Will you come back and reclaim your child, rip her away and change her name? How could we ever trust you? How could we ever believe you?

Who are you, anyhow? What kind of person would get herself knocked up by a scummy guy who runs away when he hears the news? Haven't you heard of birth control? Of AIDS? Of abortion? Of OB/GYNs? Of monogamy? Of love?

I don't want my kid to be your mistake.

Here is what we actually wrote:

Dear Birth Mother:

This must be a very difficult time for you. It takes courage to think about what would be best for your child and to choose adoptive parents for him or her.

We would like to be those lucky parents. We've been happily married for five years, but find that we are not able to have our own child. At ages 37 and 39 we would like, more than anything, to adopt an infant who would be deeply loved and well provided for in our home.

Everyone who knows us tells us we would be wonderful parents. We are playful and patient, thoughtful and artistic. We enjoy our nieces, nephews, and little friends in the neighborhood.

Within a few steps of our front door is a playground, with a pool and lots of room to run around. We live in a spacious, three-bedroom townhouse with an expansive view of the mountains. It's a healthy, happy place for kids to grow up.

We both have excellent jobs but would take off time to be with the baby. All of the grandparents, cousins, aunts, and uncles have been supportive of our adoption plans and are excited about the newest addition to the family.

We were brought up in a Jewish tradition that places great value on family, education, and kindness toward others. Though we are Caucasian, we have friends from all different backgrounds, religions, ages, and ethnic groups, and always like learning about their customs.

The happiness a child would add to our lives is matched by the happiness and love he or she would receive as part of our family. We can't wait to meet that special baby.

Thankfully, the first letter never made it past my head.

Meeting your Child's Mother

*What do you wear, what do you say,
how do you look without staring?*

I remember the date and the outfit. October 27, a Saturday; khaki slacks and a boxy linen shirt that I could have tucked in but didn't. I wanted to look good but not prissy, stylish but not overdressed. More Casual Corner than Ann Taylor. Meeting the mother of your child is like nothing else you've ever done, so you haven't the foggiest notion of how to act. All you know is that you desperately want to please and want to like this individual—an utter stranger *and* the most important person in your life.

My husband and I had gotten the call only days before—there was a birth mother in Southern California who wanted to meet us. Her name was Martina, but they called her Martie. We knew that she was eighteen years old, Mexican-American, six months' pregnant, and very sure that she was *not* going to keep the baby. That's all the information we had, except for a fax of a photograph.

It was a high-school portrait. She was staring into the camera with an attitude befitting her senior status. Uncomfortably good posture made her chin point up and her face foreshorten. From what I could tell, she had thick black hair, full lips, and raccoon eyes from too much liner. She might be pretty underneath.

The car ride from the airport to the attorney's office took too long, but it was also over too quickly. In the parking garage, I checked my hair one more time in the side mirror and took a deep breath to calm the hyperactive butterflies in my stomach. I wasn't at all sure about the difference between Mexican-American and Hispanic and had a panicky feeling that Martina/ Martie might ask.

Feliz Navidad, buenos días, Ponce de León, Cinco de Mayo, hacienda, siesta, the Alamo, Cesar Chavez, tacos, burritos, enchiladas, nachos, and adiós. That's all I knew. It was appalling. I swore that I'd learn more no matter what happened after this meeting.

Nervous laughter took the place of words when we first shook hands with Martie and her stepmother in the fourth-floor conference room. I remember the lawyer's last-minute but pointless advice: "Just be yourself." Yeah, right. I gravitated toward Martie and perched next to her on the couch but then wished I hadn't, because I couldn't see her face from the front. All I wanted to do was to stare, to memorize her face and picture it on a baby.

Against her olive-brown skin, sans high-school make-up, Martie had beautiful gray marbles for eyes and a nice, open smile. "What great teeth you have," I said, sounding too much like the Big Bad Wolf. I counted five earring studs on the ear closest to me and chalked it up to style and youth. I very much wanted to see our birth mother as a basically good girl, who was happy, popular, and smart, who had a nice family, good self-esteem, and a clear vision for her future. I wanted Martie to be a younger version of me: not perfect, but familiar. I wanted to package her pregnancy as an ill-timed mistake with a steady boyfriend, who just happened to be the star quarterback and valedictorian of his high school.

The reality was not as tidy. Though living with her parents, Martie had hidden the pregnancy from them for nearly six months (thanks to oversize men's shirts); she had gone for an abortion (too late); and her ex-boyfriend James—a handsome, eighteen-year-old biracial guy—wanted nothing to do with the pregnancy or beyond. Even though he was out of the picture, Martie described James as "really nice, funny, and caring." Caring? Nice? I wanted to challenge her choice of words but squelched the sarcasm.

Like most adoptive parents who hope to get chosen for a baby, we had put together a photo album of our lives to serve as a sales pitch to potential birth parents. Beyond the earnest narrative—"We have a loving relationship and a happy life in a beautiful environment, which we would like to share with a child"—it was actually screaming out, "Pick us, pick us, pick us."

In fact, Martie *had* picked us—at least to meet—based on those photographs and words. We sat in the lawyer's office that Saturday morning thumbing through that same photo album, sounding like the Honolulu Chamber of Commerce as we extolled the virtues of where we lived.

This, I realized, was the ultimate job interview. The young woman sitting at my side was holding our parental destiny in her hands (well, her uterus). She may have been feeling vulnerable at six months' pregnant and without a boyfriend or health insurance, but she was actually the powerful one. Where once we were supplicants to our near forty-year-old bodies, our new fertility goddess was only eighteen.

I wanted to like Martie. If you want to like a birth mother, you'll find things about her to like. And I did. She was funny, and tough, and even sweet, in spite of herself. I knew she was capable of deception, I knew she was careless about sex, I knew she still loved James. I liked her so much, I never asked about all those earrings on her left lobe.

I never asked her about her diet either, but I really wanted to know if the baby had been subsisting on pizza and chips, nachos with cheese, and Diet Coke. I wanted her to be as concerned about the baby's health as I would have been at six months' pregnant. Green, leafy vegetables might have been wishful thinking, but had she heard of prenatal vitamins? I just couldn't find a way to ask that wouldn't make me come across as some holier-than-thou macrobiotic vegan. I knew the important stuff: Martie didn't do drugs, she had quit smoking, and she wasn't ambivalent about adoption.

She never asked us about certain things, either. Like how we intended to bring up a child of a different race . . . make that different races. He/she would be half Hispanic, a quarter African-American, and a quarter Caucasian. I was relieved but uneasy that Martie didn't ask; relieved because I didn't know the right answer, uneasy because I thought she should have asked the question.

That's when it occurred to me that we were all part of an unspoken conspiracy to make it work. She needed us, we needed her. I never knew how many (if any) other adoptive families were being considered by Martie. The lawyer wouldn't say. The adoption process —casting the best light on all parties involved and putting a premium on the end product—would make a great case study for a marketing textbook. By the time you've reached the lawyer's office and have met a birth mother, you are as close to a baby as you've ever been, and you just want to close the deal.

I wasn't sure how or when we would know the verdict: A letter? A phone call? In five minutes? In two weeks? Then, I noticed that the conversation had moved from the hypothetical—when Martie's stepmother asked, "How would you tell a child about adoption?" to the more friendly and practical—when Martie wondered, "How often would you want to stay in touch?"

Before leaving the lawyer's office at noon, we knew that Martie had picked us. We picked her, too. The knowledge that Martie wanted us to parent her child —even though our skin color, religion, age, and ethnicity differed from hers—made a far-fetched match seem right. We felt a connection with her and a growing sense that this was meant to be.

Martie asked if we could fly back in January to be with her for the delivery at St. Peter's Hospital in Orange Grove, California. I hugged her as we parted and promised to speak by phone on a regular basis.

The magnitude of what had just transpired was beginning to sink in: After all those years of trying, we finally had received a positive pregnancy test. I was giddy with excitement—the kind of excitement that is infused with nervousness. In spite of Martie's assurances, I was scared about the adoption falling through . . . and just as scared about the adoption coming true.

Expecting
WITHOUT PREGNANCY

Buy the crib, but hang on to the receipt.

When you are chosen, you can almost feel yourself holding a baby. In reality, you are many, many steps away from that, so you must learn to keep your hungry arms at your side.

I wanted to tell everyone about my impending motherhood and secretly wished to be treated with the kindness and special attention bestowed on many pregnant women. Granted, no one was about to give up a seat on the bus for me, but I was hoping to be cut some slack for my distracted focus at work.

I knew it was risky to be this excited. To count so completely on something so iffy. We had heard from one adoption agency that 50 percent of all adoption matches fall through. But there was no way I could artificially cap my feelings as a protective measure against the possibility that the adoption would fail. I couldn't make myself less excited in order to cushion any devastation down the line. The only dent in my feelings of joy came from knowing, deep down, that this wasn't the real thing. It was like going to the prom with a cousin or a friend. You got to go all right, but by virtue of determination, not romance.

When Martie was seven and a half months' pregnant, I flew to visit my mother, who had offered to take me shopping for a layette. The woman behind the counter was "clued-in" quickly by my mom and never once asked about my first trimester. She guided us through the so-called "necessities," including receiving blankets, pacifiers, cloth diapers ("a million and one uses, even if you plan to use disposables"), tiny T-shirts, adorable "onesies," and even a hat. She threw in a soft clown rattle and a crib wet sheet that she thought I couldn't live without.

It was a fun and indulgent afternoon, and when we stopped for tea at a coffee shop, I felt inside of one of the images of mothers and daughters imprinted in my head. The bags at my feet were concrete evidence of my forthcoming baby. Motherhood was becoming more real to me, not by virtue of a swelling belly, but with a growing accumulation of baby stuff. I sensed the slightest whiff of pity from our baby-store guide and wondered if these gifts represented a dream come true for me and my mother, or a dream that didn't come true. Every thought of this baby to come was also a reminder of the baby that never came.

Nonetheless, my husband and I got ready for our baby with an impelling force that would hopefully stave off any second thoughts (on Martie's part and ours) by virtue of sheer momentum.

Back at home, we compared lists of baby names each of us had jotted down while I was away. Some of our best names came from scanning the credits at the end of movies, which we faithfully sat through until the popcorn sweepers arrived. By Martie's eighth month, we had narrowed the list to eleven girl's names, while not yet being able to agree on even a single boy's name.

Consciously or not, we were enacting the pregnancy. We started taking walks after dinner and getting lots of sleep. When I noticed my husband ordering whole wheat toast instead of a cinnamon bun with Sunday breakfast, I knew we were taking this seriously. Eating in a healthier way was no insurance against the adoption falling through, but it made us feel more like role models, and somehow, more like parents.

I went to check out cribs one afternoon. I never knew how many different kinds of mattresses, bumpers, and crib slats were available to infants, or if any of those really mattered. One observant salesclerk complimented me on considering such a lovely gift. Was it for my sister? Or perhaps for a good friend? I had forgotten that, in her eyes, I wasn't pregnant.

I had always felt just a little bit sorry for people I knew of who had adopted—like they were slightly underprivileged, or had had some bad luck. I wonder if that's how people thought of me and my husband now. None of our close friends had adopted, but everybody knew somebody who had. We had all heard the same horror stories—nightmares with names like Baby Jessica, Baby Richard, and Isaiah. The question we got asked most frequently was not "Have you chosen a name for the baby?" but "Aren't you afraid she'll want the baby back?"

I sat sobbing in front of CNN that August day when they came to transfer then two-and-a-half-year-old Baby Jessica from her adoptive parents to her birth parents, where she'd eventually be called "Anna" and supposedly learn to love and trust and smile again. I'm convinced that her memory of being ripped apart from her mommy and forced into a car seat screaming is forever imprinted in her psyche, no matter what her new name or address. I know it is etched in the hearts of those of us who watched in disbelief from thousands of miles away.

Rulings like this one—in favor of biology at all costs—arouse indignity in most people, sheer horror in adoptive parents, and a fear that can immobilize those who are considering adoption. So wrenching on a primal level, disrupted adoptions cast a gloom over all adoptions; they make great television, but they set the adoption movement back by years and make open adoption look deviant.

Even so, we kept on going. Whether we fantasized that we were somehow immune to such a thing, whether we truly believed Martie when she told us she was sure about her decision, or whether we were just too far along to turn back, we proceeded. And yes, I was deathly afraid that she would want the baby back. At the surprise shower thrown one Sunday afternoon, we drank champagne out of baby bottles, opened lots of pastel-colored gifts, and were toasted repeatedly by loving friends and coworkers. We were very touched and grateful for the added assurance that this thing was going to happen . . . if not now, at some point down the line. No one talked precisely about *this* baby, but about *a* baby, and I wondered if they had held on to their receipts.

In that last month, I found myself wanting to talk to the baby and looking up rather than down to do so. I could never conjure a picture of him or her, and I would never feel the kicking, but I kept talking to the baby girl or boy in another woman in another state. I found myself spending a lot of time fixing up the guest-room-turned-nursery. Sometimes I just sat there, rocking, practicing.

I couldn't believe that a little person was going to sleep in that room before long. I would fold and refold the little T-shirts and socks in the nearly empty dresser drawers and wonder how someone could be small enough to have a foot the size of a marshmallow. It all seemed a bit unreal.

Unspoken
PREFERENCES

*What matters is what you get,
not what you want.*

Adoptive parents are supposed to feel grateful for
whatever they get. That's why I didn't announce my
preference for a girl. When your baby is not coming
from your body, you tend to grope for whatever is
familiar. Growing up as one of four sisters, I knew a
lot more about periods than penises.

There was so much to hope for—that the baby
would be healthy, that Martie would be able to let go,
that we would fall in love with her offspring—that
asking for a girl seemed like pushing my luck. The
sonograms were silent on the matter of gender. Truth
is, I had no say about picking pink or blue, so I chose
lime green and stayed quiet.

Like any other would-be parents, we didn't know
if this would be a healthy baby, but unlike those who

give birth, we had the option of walking away. That option, meant to console anxious adoptive parents who have no control otherwise, was a disquieting one. It meant that my husband and I had to figure out in advance whether we would accept a baby with a birth defect, a deformity, or a disability. And if we would, how far on the continuum of ill-health would we go? Would we say yes to a cleft palate, but no to Down's syndrome? Would two missing fingers be okay but not two missing arms? Could we live with a special-needs child?

When a baby comes from your body, you take what you get and blame your own gene pool. But what person would willingly sign on for that kind of sentence? Many parents end up caring for children with cerebral palsy, deafness, heart defects, etc., but most did not choose to.

At every step of our journey toward adoption, we were being sized up as potential parents and repeatedly tested to measure the strength of our conviction. We had to answer questions that biological parents have the privilege to ignore or deal with later. The intrusively thorough application forms presented options like they were menu items—healthy, or other than healthy; white, or other than white; newborn, or other than newborn—but we knew that our responses would dictate our options. If we chose "white, healthy, new-born," our wait would be years; if we chose "other than white, less than healthy, older than newborn," we could have a baby within weeks. That, combined with the implicit message, "If you want a baby enough, you'll take whatever you get," influenced our choices.

I had to admit that I *didn't* want a child enough to suffer through a lifetime of illness, deformity, or disability. It is one thing to check no on an application; it is quite another to walk away from a living human being in need of care. An infant twice abandoned. If Martie's baby wasn't healthy, I no sooner knew if I could live with such a child than if I could live with the decision not to. I prayed that I'd never have to answer that question.

The application form was unrelenting: "Would you accept twins?" "How about a child of a race different from your own?" (We checked yes to both.) It gets even trickier when you're asked to indicate *which* races would be "acceptable": Asian, Native American, Hispanic, African-American, mixed, etc. Answering any of these questions exacts an honesty that is brutal. You are forced to face any prejudices you might have— from mongoloid faces to flat noses, from kinky hair to stuttered speech—even if you've never owned up to them.

Many Caucasian adoptive parents are initially looking for white, healthy newborns; some have the audacity to order custom-designed babies. I saw one ad that read: *"Blue-eyed, blonde-haired couple looking to provide healthy U.S. infant with Christian values and much love."* My suspicion is that adoptive parents who want their adoptive children to match may not be ready to adopt at all. Or maybe they are ethnocentric. Or maybe they're just smarter than I am. Perhaps they've actually thought through the long-term impacts and concluded that life is simpler when kids look like their parents, tougher when they don't, and roughest when neither their faces nor their races match.

For those who are willing to cross the color line with an interracial adoption, there is another decision: this one so distasteful, it's often avoided. A shameless discussion about skin pigmentation—how dark is too dark—often reveals an unconscionable preference for yellow over brown, for brown over black, for light over dark. There are many more Asian babies than African-American babies adopted by Caucasian parents; as if the yellow-white combination is less interracial than the black-white one.

We knew we wanted a healthy newborn, but we didn't feel a strong need to be matched by race or features. Our willingness to parent a child of a different race had more to do with naïveté than with altruism. We weren't sufficiently aware of the repercussions of adopting transracially to have been proactive advocates for that option. We didn't understand that we might be taking on a job even bigger than parenting . . . that of transmitting a culture that was not ours. We simply knew that we wanted a baby, we believed that we would be good parents, and we presumed we could love in any color. We also thought we could love in any shade. Naïveté served us well in expediting our application and expanding our adoption options.

EXCITEMENT
OR DOOM?

*There's a thin line between
being thrilled and being nauseated.*

We considered Martie's invitation to be in the delivery
room a once-in-a-lifetime opportunity and one that we'd
never risk missing. That's why we flew to California a
week before her due date. Three and a half weeks
later, living out of a hotel room, leashed to a cellular
phone . . . this was no vacation. That Martie had
guessed wrong on the date of conception came as a
surprise only by comparison to my precise knowledge
of my daily basal temperature and menstrual cycle.

"Well?" "So?" Well-meaning friends and family
members called to ask, even after assurances that we
would call them with any news. "At least you don't
have to wait the whole nine months," they consoled,
when, in fact, we had been waiting years by this time.

About two weeks into our hotel-room life, we were

invited to meet Martie's family. I think they felt sorry for us. These strangers would actually be related to us in some unorthodox way and a part of our lives forever. I knew that meeting them would be a great opportunity and a chance to learn more about our child's heritage. But that didn't make it easy. This open adoption stuff was scary.

The directions to the family home in Huntington Park were very clear; so clear, that we arrived too early and rode around the block a few times. We knocked at the prescribed hour and were greeted at the door by Martie. Looking over her shoulder as we hugged, I saw a room full of people staring at me. They turned out to be brothers and sisters with spouses and names like Carmen, Kathleen, and Tina; J.J., Paul, and Doug. Martie's baby might have had an Aunt Tina, an Uncle J.J., and a Grandpa John, but instead would have a Nana Bess, an Aunt Sophie, and a cousin Daniella.

All eleven of us piled into four cars and caravaned to Pizza Time, where someone ordered five pizzas and pitchers of Coke. (Martie, I noticed, went for the pepperoni with double cheese.) Everyone was friendly, including Martie's dad, who, we had heard, was the toughest of all silent judges. Our conversation was about airplane food, HOV lanes, and big families; it was not about pregnancy, adoption, or loss. In its far-reaching and quip-filled banter, the visit was about as normal as could be under circumstances that were anything but normal.

We knew we'd see Martie and her stepmom at the hospital soon, but we said good-bye to the others without knowing when, if ever, we'd see them again. Back at our hotel-home, we wondered why no one from this big and friendly family had come forward to adopt the baby.

Everything we did, we did with the sense that it could be the very last time. Our last full night of sleep. Our last romantic dinner. A last chance to read a trashy novel or talk on the phone in peace. I felt like I was about to lose all that I knew. Nothing would ever be the same. The trickles of excitement about the baby could be very quickly dashed by waves of anxiety. A feeling of "impending doom" doesn't exactly describe it, but it's close. A pregnant woman might feel the same way, but her status transition—from self-focused woman to baby-focused mother—could be more gradual. I, on the other hand, could run a marathon or fly cross-country the day before becoming a mother.

I looked up a few of the people I knew in Southern California. That they all had kids was both good and bad. Good if the kids didn't join us when we got together. That way, these already-mothers could tell me that my life *would* even out; that it's ultimately worth all the hard stuff; that it might even be a little fun; that I would feel love like I never had before. On the other hand, if their kids were there, I could see for myself the reality of mustard diapers, the run-after-me-if-you-want-me-to-get-in-the-car-seat game, the crying for good reasons and then no reasons, the not-so-cute (except to their parents) faces, the massive amount of luggage that gets packed for a simple little outing to the park.

There were times during our long wait when I worried that this was a bad decision. Maybe people who can't have babies shouldn't have babies. Maybe people who can have babies should stay with them. Maybe this baby inside of Martie wasn't showing up for a good reason.

Waiting, when you know you've got a lot of it, is barely tolerable. Waiting, when you don't have much longer, is unbearable. Your mind does funny things, like assigning spiritual significance to the smallest and most mundane occurrences. A cloudy day, a Fisher Price recall . . . maybe we should call it off. With each non–birth day that passed, I shed a little more of the confidence and patience I had shown in our pre-adoption interviews.

I had absolutely no control over a situation that

would impact my life profoundly and irreversibly. I was stuck between wanting something in a powerful way and wanting to walk away from its power: like sitting with a toothache in the waiting room of a dentist who is running very late. You want to walk out in protest over a lack of respect for your schedule, but you need to get your throbbing tooth fixed.

I would give this kid one more week.

Martie and I were both waiting—only she was waiting for it to be over, and I was waiting for it to begin. A split screen might have shown Martie watching *Oprah* from a sofa in her living room, while I was watching *Oprah* from a StairMaster in the hotel's fitness center. We were two illegitimate mothers of one illegitimate baby—each of us slightly defective by society's standards. Maybe we'd talk about it one day on *Oprah*.

Like a full-fledged schizophrenic, I loved Martie for the gift that was coming, and I utterly resented her for doing what I couldn't. Our female bodies had all the same parts—vagina, uterus, and fallopian tubes—but hers worked and mine didn't. Giving birth should have been a basic right of mine: solace for years of menstrual cramps and stockpiles of Tampax under my bathroom sink. Payback for all of the condoms, foam, diaphragms, and birth control pills that had protected my sex in high school, through college, and during my single days (which could have been more swinging, had I only known). Recompense for the needles, the pills and the bills, the cold examination rooms, the gloved fingers up my cervix, the waiting—month after endless month —for my chemically confused body to follow orders.

Martie had been a bad girl: she screwed around, got drunk, and relied on luck for birth control. I had been good: not Goody Two-shoes, but at least I had an ice chip in her mouth, Martie was looking tired and pissed-off. Was she mad at us? At her escaped boyfriend? At the doctor? At the baby? I felt downright guilty that she was going through all of this only to go home empty-handed. Her back hurt, she was thirsty, she wanted to get it over with. I could sense the bubble over her head shouting: *Get me out of this place; I hate all of you.*

The injustice. I wore a long teal turtleneck sweater over black stirrup pants and a favorite pair of silver earrings. Martie wore a bluish gown partly covered with hard white sheets that had "Property of St. Peter's Hospital" printed on the top and bottom—as if someone would actually want to steal them. I wanted to apologize to Martie, but I had to remind myself that it wasn't my fault; I certainly hadn't gotten her pregnant.

By 11:00 A.M. Martie was not even three centimeters dilated and was desperate to get to the magic number four, when the nurses would give her an epidural. Between contractions, we slipped ice chips into Martie's mouth, held her hand, made limp jokes about not getting the minimum wage for such hard labor, and waited. By midafternoon, we were sent by the nurses to the hospital cafeteria for lunch. Stale saltines. Every time the paging system squeaked before a mumbled announcement, we froze and strained to make out our names, as if waiting to be called for an execution.

Because Martie asked us to attend the birth, the hospital insisted that we first watch a seventy-five-minute videotape on vaginal delivery. I sat in the overheated library at St. Peter's, staring at images of an actual birth, all the time thinking: "This is disgusting —can we go now?" If Martie had seen this, she'd be out of here; this gory little horror movie would have put her over the edge. For having sat through the video on those wooden classroom chairs (the ones with the wide arms for taking notes, which we didn't), we earned a little white slip of paper signed by librarian *S. Grabowsky*. No quiz, no questions.

I could never do what our birth mother was about to do—both relinquish her baby and invite an audience to view the birth. Both are acts of enormous generosity, incredible strength. By comparison, I was a full-blown wimp. Funny how our friends saw us as "courageous" and "risk takers." To me, Martie was the *real* hero.

I felt a kind of closeness with Martie that comes from changing together in a locker room. I had seen her pubic hair, for God's sake, and we had talked about her mucous plug. The intimacy of sharing in her labor could bond us for life, and yet, Martie was a foreigner to me—a different species who had the ability to give birth then choose not to parent. I could not fathom the very transaction that was bestowing me a child. I could never let go of a being that my body had housed and nourished for nine months, and I did not fully understand someone who could.

The waiting continued. Another meal in the hospital cafeteria. The turkey sandwiches from lunch had been transformed into turkey salad for dinner. Like the day's menu, the hours seemed to dissolve, one into the next.

By 7:00 P.M., I thought they'd call the whole thing off on account of either darkness or extreme tardiness. Martie was miserable, her stepmother was edgy, I was queasy with intermittent numbness. The white-coated Dr. Lerman finally appeared. Stitched in blue script letters above his pocket behind his pens was *M. Lerman, M.D.* My guess was *Maurice,* but it might have been *Martin.* Definitely not a *Mike* or a *Mac;* he was the crankiest of anyone. He threw a "Hello" to Martie, ignored my husband and me, and barked at the nurses from inside a thick file-folder where his face landed: "I told you to start the Pitocin as soon as she got in! Why the hell did you wait until 7:00 in the morning? I can't stay all night, you know." *Excuuuse* us. Don't you think Martie's had a little harder time today than you, Doctor?

We were all stuck there, in that room, and we all wanted the same thing for different reasons: We wanted out.

Sixteen hours after entering the hospital, Martie

was ready to deliver. My husband and I stood on one side of her bed, Martie's stepmother and a nurse on the opposite side—like four pallbearers. The doctor stood ready to catch at the foot of the bed, and the masked anesthesiologist floated somewhere near Martie's head.

I was vertical when I should have been horizontal. *I* was the one who should have been lying on my back with my legs up. Standing was for husbands and midwives, not mothers. The searing pain of my infertility came back to stab me once again. It attacked in intervals, like Martie's contractions, but she was the only one screaming.

With her knees up, Martie's belly mound seemed smaller already. "Push!" the white coat yelled. I thought he was obnoxious and wanted to tell him so, but I didn't want to get kicked out or, worse, have the whole adoption fall through on account of my candor.

I decided I'd get through this experience by watching another woman have her baby, not by watching another woman have mine.

I held Martie's hand, counted while she pushed, and frankly, didn't know where to look. I wanted to encourage her with my eyes, but they desperately wanted to travel southward to check out her vagina, which was launching a wet, black-haired head into the world. Was it rude to look? I doubt the etiquette books address this dilemma.

I didn't just look, I stared. If I was being gauche, I couldn't help it. Birth is a miracle, an incredible sight that most mothers never see. The amazement was not that this was *my* baby, but that any human being could come out of that dark hole. This was *National Geographic* come alive. Stretching to hold Martie's hand (as if to say, "I still care about you"), I craned my neck around her bent knee to get an even better view.

The baby seemed stuck in the birth canal. No wonder . . . they had given Martie a shot of morphine for pain moments earlier, and she just couldn't push any more. I saw thick, matted hair on the crown of an infant's head and thought, "Oh my God, here she comes!" Then Dr. Lerman tried to suction the baby and, when that failed, sent us out of the room so that we wouldn't see the barbaric forceps latch onto the forehead as he forcibly yanked the baby into the world.

I had one last chance to make a getaway—to run down the hall and disappear back into a safer life. Within seconds, though, the door was reopened, my husband and I were ushered in, and my eyes met Martie's. I knew it was over, but I didn't know the ending. She turned and, without expression, escorted my eyes to our child, on a small table where nurses were huddled. All I saw was a naked, brown blur. Some-body yelled, "It's a boy!" and I heard a wail. There I was, staring, being stared at, and crying for reasons that others saw only as happiness.

With a swollen right eye and red-brown gravy still in his hair, the infant looked like he had been in a fight, as if we had interrupted him in the middle of some-thing. He didn't look like my baby, and I worried silently about that.

His first Apgar test score—based on a quick physical given to all newborns—was only a four out of ten; that's like scoring a C– on the very first exam of your life. It scared me, though the nurses said they would retest for respiration and heartbeat. Was this baby defective, or was he just exhausted, having traveled minutes earlier through a very rough passage? I couldn't help but wonder what his score would have been if he had come out of me, but felt elitist for letting that thought in. I hoped no one could read my mind.

Because he hadn't come out of me, I was allowed to think what would be unthinkable to a mother who had given birth. I had a horrible option: an escape clause. The concept of returning damaged goods was repugnant to me: What right did I have to demand a perfect child? Here was a living being, perfect in his own way. I didn't love him yet, but I could never walk away from him.

Martie managed a smile. We went to her bedside while they were vacuuming the baby, and, like a trouper, she said she was "okay." Morphine helped to make Martie numb that night at the hospital; the real and the surreal induced the same effect in me. I rubbed Martie's shoulder, held her hand, and, at that moment, was in touch with the utter unnaturalness of adoption. That this being had come out of Martie's body, but would not stay a part of her, no longer made sense to me.

IF THIS IS THE HAPPIEST DAY OF MY LIFE, WHY AM I SO SAD?

The myth of bliss.

A baby! I knew this was supposed to be the happiest day of my life, and that made me feel even worse. This was nothing like I pictured. What about those images of exhausted, beaming, brand-new mothers holding tiny infants to their bloated chests? This wasn't that. And how about those kittens born in my childhood closet, or those baby robins in their nest, or those puppies squirming underneath their mommy dog? *That* was natural; this was something else.

I went first to Martie—whom I had known now for three months—before going to the baby—whom I had just met. As special as it was to witness this birth, I could do nothing to soften its hard reality: I had been there, I had seen it, and I could never pretend that this baby had arrived by magic, in joyful unambivalence. I could never look at him without seeing her. His presence in my life meant his absence in hers. Would he ever feel like my baby, or would he always feel like someone else's? I wasn't at all sure that this was meant to be. The destiny I had earlier read into this scenario was nowhere to be found the night of his birth day.

"He's so dark," I thought, and felt ashamed for thinking it. But he was. I expected black hair, but I had also expected olive skin, like Martie's. My racist gut reaction was fueled by gut fear. I was pretty sure I had taken on more than I could handle. Adoption of a white kid would have been enough of a stretch, but we had to go for a baby that not only came out of someone else's body, but out of someone else's culture. What were we thinking? What kind of pseudo–Peace Corps types were we pretending to be? All I could think of was that we were too white to be the parents of someone this black.

And where was the baby girl that the sonograms had promised? The girl whom I'd been calling "Mira," as in miracle, in my silent, daily talks with her these past few months. I was looking for her the night that Martie's son was born; I was so sure she was coming. When she turned out to be a he, I wept not only for Mira, but also for the daughter I never had, and for the baby with light skin, as if I had known them all.

The nurses had never witnessed such a tearful outpouring of happiness on the part of an adoptive mother. Their misreading gave me a chance to catch my sobbing breath and regain some level of composure, if only in the form of numbness. I simply didn't know what to work on first. I'd better adjust to having a baby, I had to accept that he was a boy, I needed to get used to dark brown skin, and I'd better come up with a name for this kid—and all before someone caught on to my feelings of pure panic.

WHY THIS BABY?

Of all the babies born tonight,
how did you get us?
Of all the people wanting a baby,
how did we get you?

My husband and I slipped into oversize white gowns, then washed our hands conscientiously with pink liquid soap and put on surgical masks. After all that, the perinatal nurses let us carry a beaten-up, dirty camera bag into the newborn nursery.

How funny/strange/wonderful/weird that, out of all the babies born that Monday night at St. Peter's Hospital, *this* was the one who would come home with us.

It wasn't the tiny Korean baby girl with the thick black hair; nor the screaming, bald infant, red from crying; nor the twin Hispanic boys sleeping soundly. It was the alert, 8.2-pound, 21-inch boy lying quietly on his back, with both eyes open. On his tiny chest, a gold, heart-shaped sticker, holding in place a miniature heart monitor. Under a white, powdery frosting, I could see his flawless brown skin. He was completely sweet and utterly foreign. No one would ever mistake him as my child.

It made me wince to see his swollen eye and to know that he had been hurt so early on in his life. I looked at him; he looked somewhere else.

I wish it had been love at first sight. It was more like pity at first sight. This newborn had neither a name nor parents, for the moment. He would sleep as an orphan tonight. His little life was already so complicated, and he was only minutes old.

I stroked him, awkwardly, with no practice to rely on. He was doughy; my fingers felt bony and cold. I wondered how we, an unlikely combination, ended up together. Of all the people wanting a child, how did we get you, baby boy? And how did you get us? By virtue of a piece of paper that your mother signed, I have the right to be with you in this, your first half-hour of life, to touch you, to watch your very first sponge bath. You had absolutely no say in the matter. You did not invite me into your bassinet, much less into your life. Maybe that's why I am feeling like an impostor, like an intruder, like I haven't really earned the right to be here.

I don't feel much like a mother, and I don't feel anything like *his* mother. I try to remind myself that

Martie chose us to parent her child. She picked *me* to be her baby's mother. Even so, the match feels forced.

There are no external commonalties confirming our linkage, either. I am not Hispanic; not African-American; not Californian; not male. I have nothing in common with this baby except for the air in the room and the possibility that we could end up together in the same family.

If it all works out, I'll tell myself it was meant to be. If it doesn't work out, I'll tell myself it was meant to be.

How different would his life be, would his personality be, his religion and even his name, growing up as the child of an eighteen-year-old, single, Hispanic woman living in Huntington Park, California? How much of who he is will be coming home with us, and how much will he be leaving behind? We'll never know, but we'll always wonder.

A FAMILY OF STRANGERS

Related, but not relatives.

From behind the baby's clear plastic bassinet in the newborn nursery, I looked across a large observation window into the corridor and saw a family of strangers —each intent on taking in the sight of the same infant. My mom and dad, just flown in and still holding their coats, were memorizing their grandson on the very first view. Martie, having been sewn up, stopped the gurney that was headed to her hospital room, to get a good look at the son she had given birth to thirty minutes earlier. Standing behind her were Martie's stepmom and sister, propping up each other. Their transfixed eyes were dulled with exhaustion and gave no hint of the swirling emotions that, I know, inflicted us all.

The two grandmothers—my mother and Martie's—

stood side by side, but they would never meet. Their shoulders were parallel but their lives were not, as they shared in the arrival and departure of a new grandson.

The next time I looked up, some of them were gone. As if their time were up, Martie and her family disappeared into the hospital. My parents stood there for a long time afterward, throwing kisses automatically. The smile on my mother's face seemed to start each time I looked up from the baby and dissolve each time I looked down. This can't be what she dreamed of when I walked down the aisle.

THE NAME GAME

*Should we name him after my family,
your family, or her family?*

By the time we were back at the hospital early the next morning, standing at the bank of phone booths on the OB floor, we had slept three hours and agreed on a name for the little boy whom we'd met for the first time the night before.

Less than twelve hours old, he showed himself to be both strong and peaceful: that's why we named him "Ari," which means lion in Hebrew, and "Yona," which means dove.

Even though the name seemed to fit, I felt a little embarrassed telling Martie and her family that we had chosen "Ari" instead of "Stephen" or "Michael" or "William" or "Christopher." We were afraid that an unfamiliar name (even worse, a Hebrew name) would remind her of how different our world was from hers, of how different her son's world would be from his mother's. I braced myself and thought, "Take him now, if you're going to change your mind."

For the original birth certificate, Martie would write "Gary Robert," the middle names of her two brothers. She had informed us when we met her that the choice of names was ours, and that she didn't much care (though I suspect she had never heard of an "Ari"). "Cool," she said when she heard it, as if it were her second choice. Most of the time, I referred to him as "the baby," because I was no more used to hearing his name than Martie.

Loving Before It's Legal

Parenting without permission.

He slept through most of the day, but I think we were beginning to bond—at least I was. I stared at him long enough to remember his face when I left for the bathroom or cafeteria. He wasn't sucking any formula, and I thought he must be getting pretty hungry. He was also pretty shaky, but I didn't know how much of that was normal. I thought it was a good sign that I was worried.

I knew from the frequent visits of nurses, doctors, and orderlies that something might be wrong with the baby. When we asked, they offered only scraps: "Well, we're just checking on his jaundice," or, "We're making sure his eye is doing okay," or, "Let's just get an X-ray of this clavicle to be sure." To be sure of what? I didn't know whether they were holding back because the news was bad or because we, not yet legal parents, had no right to be consulted about these things.

I may not have been his legal parent, I may not have felt qualified even to be a parent at that point . . . but I knew I had feelings for this tiny guy when I watched blood get taken from his sticklike arm. I didn't know him well enough to "feel" his needle empathically, but I cared enough to recoil when he got poked and tear up at his helplessness. The orderly worked right through the baby's screaming, never stopping to soothe him or make him more comfortable. I wanted to strangle the guy with his white lab coat, grab my almost-son, and run.

It was really scary, and we, as this baby's potential adoptive parents, were nobodies in the hospital system. We had no advocates, and worse, we couldn't advocate for the baby who might become our son. I am ashamed by the small comfort I got in watching a cocaine-addicted newborn in the next bassinet cry the day away. At least "our" baby wasn't that miserable.

I kept rocking my new little friend—awkwardly, of course. I'm sure I held him too far from my chest, not wanting to disappoint his routing mouth with a useless breast. I told him about us, half hoping he'd sit up, unwrap his bunting, and give me the A-okay sign, as if he knew everything was going to be fine.

We took turns holding him. At first, I was relieved to relinquish my duty and would hope that, if he cried, he'd do it on my husband's watch. By the next day, I noticed that I would wait for my turn to come. "I'll take him if you're tired," I'd say to my husband— disguising my request as an offer.

The hours passed. We'd change a diaper, try a bottle, watch him. As the wall clock ticked away the day, we were getting to know him better, and getting closer to the time when Martie would be offered the final adoption papers to sign.

The morning after Ari was born, we were met in the nursery by a thirty-something female pediatrician and a social worker. My husband and I were asked to sit down so that the professionals could "break" the news to us that this appeared to be a dark baby with African-American features and ethnicity: "Were you aware of this and is that going to be a problem?" queried this concerned pediatrician.

Inside, we wanted to answer with a resounding, "Duuuuuhhhh. We thought the kid would be a lemon-haired albino." We were too proud to admit that we were initially shocked, and too shocked to think through how we were going to deal with it, but we somehow assured her that our eyes were wide open. (Sleep deprivation or truth?) The pediatrician left with a warning that babies get darker as they get older.

We were being counseled by well-meaning, white health professionals who assumed that, once we knew this baby would look black, we wouldn't want him. That kind of racism was more offensive than my own. Their message that morning: "It's not too late."

In fact, it *was* too late.

Saying Good-bye

*Even the right decisions
can feel wrong.*

Adoption involves saying good-bye to dreams, hopes, and real people. One woman says good-bye to her baby. Another woman says good-bye to her dream of giving birth. The two say good-bye to each other but stay invisibly linked as mothers to their common child.

He was born Monday night. By Tuesday, Martie signed initial forms that would allow us to take pictures of the baby and plan to leave the hospital with him on Wednesday. The birth mother would not be presented with the adoption documents for at least seventy-two hours—long enough for the anesthesia to wear off and the reality to start setting in. Even if Martie signed the relinquishment papers, we'd have to wait several more days for permission to fly home with the baby—long enough for the interstate compact forms to be received, approved, and filed 2,500 miles and three time zones away.

At Martie's request, the twelve-hour-old baby boy was brought up in a bassinet to his mother's room at the end of the hall on the second floor. There, we were told, Martie and her family would take time to look at him, hold him, snap pictures, and somehow ready themselves for good-bye. For the first time in the entire process, I worried that she'd change her mind. Why had I believed that she could go through with it? How could a mother hold her infant son, remember his face, rock his tiny body, and then let go?

We returned to the hospital only hours after leaving it at 2:30 A.M. and were disappointed to find the baby missing from the newborn nursery. We had rushed back to give him his early bottle but learned that Martie had taken care of that. She chose not to breast-feed her son, but she still wanted to feed him. The social worker suggested we grab a cup of coffee from the basement cafeteria, but we sat instead in the nursery, waiting. With my coat still on, I didn't know if I was one day away from having a baby or one day away from losing one. A floor above us was a baby who could be our son, and his mother who would decide our fate and his. It was torturous.

The bassinet arrived an hour later, and in it, a sleeping infant. We rose as if to bolster ourselves. "She'd like another visit with him this afternoon," daggered the nurse.

The three of us—not yet a family—were escorted to a room next to the nursery where cases of Isomil and stacks of pamphlets served as our coatracks and foot-rests. Without a hospital bed to call our own, we were homeless. Nurses were busying themselves around us . . . sorting through surgical masks and filling up the soap spout with antibacterial pink liquid. We shed our coats, donned our green hospital scrub suits, and took pictures of each other watching a sleeping baby. All you could see were our eyes, but they were enough.

Some time after noon, the baby was once again summoned by Martie. This time, we headed for the basement cafeteria. What could she and her family be doing up there? They must be falling in love with him by now. I remembered over lukewarm soup that it's healthy for a birth mother to see her child before letting go, but I couldn't fathom how spending more time would make it easier. How would she know when it was time for a last kiss, a last touch, a last look? How could she ever be "ready"?

I was trying to fall in love with this baby, but I didn't want to fall any further if he wasn't coming home with us. "If she wants him, she should take him right now,"

I humphed to my husband, who knew I didn't mean it. The more desperate I felt, the more indignant I sounded.

I had to remind myself that wanting to see the baby did not equate to wanting to keep the baby. Some of the books I'd read described birth mothers deliberately handing over the baby to adoptive mothers. Martie had no interest in that kind of ceremony; she never asked to see us with her son. I would have done whatever she wanted to make it easier, and I sensed that what she wanted was to be left alone.

On Wednesday morning, Martie finally asked to see us. This time, the baby stayed behind in his bassinet home in the newborn nursery, while we traveled stealthily toward Martie's semi-private room. A bouquet of helium balloons belied the heaviness in the air. She was sitting in one of those chairs where pipe-smoking dads read newspapers—with a footrest for her slippered feet. She looked slumped and sacklike in a Lanz nightgown and kindly offered a small smile. Martie said she was doing "okay" when we asked and agreed that the baby was sweet.

As if to ward off any bad news, I blurted something about a promise to take very good care of her baby and let him know about his first mother and father. We handed Martie a small gift that we had carefully selected and wrapped weeks earlier and worlds away, before we left home. Small garnet earrings would represent Martie's January birthstone and what was supposed to have been the baby's too . . . except that he didn't arrive until February. I don't think she really cared about the symbolism or cared for the style; she was much too exhausted to fake it.

Even though Martie had signed some of the pre-adoption documents, we still didn't know if we could "keep" her baby. Every happy step was dampened by the threat of the next step and the sad reality of the current one. I told Martie that we'd never forget her and never let her son forget her. That's when she told us—in a flat voice, looking somewhere else—that she had signed all the papers, that we'd be leaving the hospital with the baby that day, and she'd be leaving the day after.

I was so ready to despise Martie for changing her mind, and now all I felt was sympathy. And shame, for assuming the worst. But she *didn't* change her mind, even after holding the baby, even after feeding him. What flashed through my mind was far short of grateful: "What's wrong with this baby?" "Is there something she knows that I don't?" "How else could she do it?" I thought to myself. Martie was letting us take her child. She had said that she would and she did. I was stunned by her integrity, almost confused by her clarity. For God's sake, she was only eighteen.

I knew that we would see Martie again; but, by that time, our lives, which had crossed in such an intimate way, would once again be further apart. I also knew that the baby she gave birth to might not know Martie the next time we met. She felt awful about leaving the baby I felt awful about taking.

Most adoptive parents live with some anxiety about the birth mother changing her mind. Many adoptive mothers can understand why she would. The grief of adoption is not lost on the woman who brings the baby home.

I felt what I guess was love for Martie—not just for what she was giving us, but for who she was. She was unimaginably brave, unexplainably sure. All she asked for was a letter and pictures when we got home. Before leaving her hospital room, my husband and I took turns hugging Martie, crying, and mumbling kind words without saying "good-bye."

Downstairs, outside the nursery, we signed more papers as nurses covered the baby's soft head in a light-blue cap and wrapped him like an ice-cream cone in blankets. I wanted to leave right away, as if by leaving, we could put it all behind us. A volunteer was called to bring up a wheelchair for the discharged mother. I refused to pretend to the outside world that I had given birth to the baby I was holding; I would not sit in the throne. Since it is a liability-driven law that the person holding the baby must be pushed in a wheel-chair, my husband took the baby bundle and sat down. The stunned look of our well-intentioned, blue-coated, elderly volunteer is forever captured in a snapshot taken on our way out through the hospital lobby.

COMING HOME

Everything old seems new;
everything new seems foreign.

Even with the added height of his powder-blue ski cap, Ari practically disappeared into the car seat. I thought it looked strange to make a newborn sit up, but they don't make car seats that can strap an infant in the fetal position. My husband drove away from the hospital very tentatively, like you do just after you've gotten your permit or just after you've been stopped by a cop who lets you off with a stern warning. Everything old was new.

I kept looking toward the backseat to make sure there was still a baby with us. He didn't exist three days ago, and now he was here for good. Just because I had wanted a baby all these years didn't mean I was ready for him. I didn't have nine months to feel him inside —not a cramp, not a single kick to warn me. Not only was this stranger staying in my home, but he needed to be fed, and changed, and held, and probably a lot of other things I didn't know about as yet. It was very strange and disconcerting to be an instantaneous parent.

I may have had a lot of emotional catching up to do, but I had no free time in which to do it. Any minute there might be a scream that means something important in newborn talk—maybe a hungry mouth or a wet bottom . . . or something worse. That frantic crying seemed to have a direct line to my heart rate, sounding just as panicky as I felt. I suffered from the same malaise as many first-time parents, especially those who are older, who don't want their long-awaited kids to have to wait for anything.

Our first home as a three-day-old family was a hotel room, complete with nothing but a king-size bed, a sink, a Bible, a TV, and a stocked bar. I needed to figure out how to mix formula, sterilize nipples, and get the bubbles out, all without a kitchen and all before even figuring out how best to hold a baby.

For his trip "home" to the hotel, we dressed Ari in a unisex green romper, patterned with a circus train: more silly than cute when you tried to open the rice-sized buttons. Once inside our hotel room, we stripped Ari of his "party" clothes, projecting that he might be more comfortable in the equivalent of a T-shirt and jeans. Trying to dress or undress an infant, who you think is as fragile as porcelain, is not easy for two grown people who had previously experimented with only a plastic doll. It was wonderfully scary to feel his tiny arms and long fingers, to see how perfectly in place all the pieces were, only in miniature.

We must have stared for several hours while Ari lay unassumingly in the middle of an unmade bed. The three rolls of film my husband had taken since Ari's birth were ready to be developed, and I jumped at the chance to take a break. (So soon? What if I had had an episiotomy? No errand running then.) I drove the car to Fox One-Hour Photo just the same as I had always driven. I walked the same way. Talked to the clerk the same way. Yet, everything, everything had changed.

There would still be a baby up on that bed when I returned. It wouldn't be just two of us. The baby would still be there tonight, when we went to sleep, and tomorrow (or later tonight) when we woke up. What time it was, even what day it was, seemed to have no relevance. The only thing of any significance was getting ready for whatever Ari's next cry meant.

I took the long way around, so that my trip back to the hotel would take an extra five minutes. At that moment, I was so awed by the irreversible and enormous responsibility of being Ari's parent that I thought I could justify taking five. I could never hop in the car again and just run out for an errand. From now on, I'd have to make some "arrangement." Never did something so mundane as an errand to the store seem so filled with freedom.

An hour later, my husband would get the same opportunity. Why we needed our pictures in one hour when Ari was in the same position on the bed, wearing the same clothes and expression as when the most recent photos were shot, I am not sure. I think we needed to put a marker on this otherwise timeless and placeless afternoon and evening.

I was afraid about a lot of things in those first few days. One of them was not whether Martie would change her mind. Even in her saddest moments that last day in the hospital, and in spite of my imagining the worst, Martie was unwavering in following through with the adoption. For this, we were spared the enormous burden of uncertainty that other adoptive parents endure. I was not afraid that Martie would change her mind. I was afraid that I would.

Knowing how cranky and babyish I get when my fundamental needs for food and sleep are lacking, I worried about my capacity to be the grown-up in such a situation.

When Ari started whimpering at about 2:00 A.M., I thought, "Here goes." Just before Ari's birth, a friend warned me: "Once you have children, you will never sleep the same." "Even after the first year?" I pleaded. "Yes," said my soothsayer, ". . . for the rest of your life." Ugh. That sinking feeling again.

We breathed big sighs of tired and happy relief when our lawyer called our room to report that the papers were signed and the documents were filed. Finally, with a five-week hotel bill and a five-day-old baby, we were allowed to go home.

For the first time ever, we got to board the plane early when the announcement was made at our gate: "Individuals in need of assistance and families with young children may board at this time." For the five-hour flight home, we packed for a week: bottles, cloth diapers, disposable diapers, pacifiers, wipes, thermometer, aspirator, change of clothes, hat, sweater, socks, rattle, Penelope Leach's parenting book, and receiving blankets (sounds like they're going to make a thirty-yard pass with the kid). The amount of stuff you need to carry for a baby is not mentioned in the baby books as one of the major side effects of parenting.

We carried the baby into our house as a new bride is lifted across the threshold. We showed him all around . . . especially his very own room, which we had assembled over a month before with love and anticipation. He fell asleep on a blanket near the sliding glass door in the living room; we sat and watched, as if each of his breaths were interesting. The house began to smell of baby, and pacifiers dotted every room. We slept and ate in between cries and let the answering machine run interference.

Back in a familiar place, not one thing felt the same.

FAMILY TREES
WITHOUT ROOTS

Hoping blood isn't thicker than water.

Both my parents and my husband's were supportive of our decision to adopt, but they were clearly nervous for us. They had heard the same horror stories we had about birth mothers changing their minds and birth parents coming back for their children years later. When they heard that the baby we were waiting for was not white, their anxiety changed its focus. The gist of most of their questions was, "Are you sure you know what you're getting into?" The gist of most of our answers was, "We think so."

As the thought of an adopted grandchild from another race took hold, their questions became more dicey and their warnings more revealing. When one relative shared the perspective that "The baby may be only 25 percent black, but that doesn't mean he'll *look* only 25 percent black," my husband and I had the belated revelation that, as much as we would love the approval of our extended families, we didn't actually need it. Family discussions were restructured to focus on our news, not their views. In time, once they realized that we were going ahead with this adoption, all four prospective adoptive grandparents said to us in one way or another: "We will love your child, wherever she comes from and whatever he looks like." Significant pause. "But the world is still a racist place, and you may be making your life, and your child's life, a lot tougher." (And, I suppose, their lives, too.)

Would they really love our child as much as the grandchildren in picture frames scattered throughout their homes? Would he get a savings bond like all the others? Would they show off his baby photo as grandparents do? Would they always describe him as their "*adopted grandson*"? Would he be more like a grandson-in-law than a flesh-and-blood grandson? Would he ever blend completely, or would he always be treated like someone with a foreign accent? And would he be watched more closely than his cousins for signs of differentness?

I had few clues for knowing how my parents would be with my child. I had had a black boyfriend in college, but my mom and dad saw it for the fling that it was. I knew they were liberal thinkers and supporters of causes like the National Conference of Christians and Jews, the United Negro Fund, Displaced Homemakers of America, and Neighborhood Legal Services. But sending in a generous check, or serving Thanksgiving dinner at a soup kitchen, or hosting summer students from Nigeria, was different from burping a new grandson, or brushing his hair with a pick, or investing in his future. I wanted to know that they could love my son, but I knew that their "yes" could only be theoretical before he arrived.

Ari was a magnet for desirous hands and arms and fingers. He was lovingly pawed by too many people, both those who had a claim—like grandparents, cousins, and close friends—and those who thought they did—neighbors, acquaintances, even strangers. There were people I had never seen, whose names I never knew, who would kiss my new son's forehead or rub his little stomach. Did I have to share him, just because he was shared with me?

The baby gropers had different reasons for being eager. Both sets of grandparents just wanted to find a way to connect with their unfamiliar grandson. Like calling themselves "Nana" and "Poppy" for the first time, they had to spend time getting used to themselves with him. He was neither the first grandchild

nor the first grandson, but Ari was touched and talked
about with the gingerness of first-timers. At only two
months old, this unassuming baby represented their
greatest hopes and their biggest fears for the future: "I
want to be around long enough to see who he becomes"
said one relative, as if taking bets on some experimental
hybrid. Being adopted and being of color changed
the way this baby was held and welcomed by his new
extended family.

Young cousins, ranging in age from one to twelve, let
their hands and words do what some of the grown-ups
had self-censored themselves from doing. They explored
his hair and skin, as if either might feel different from
their own. They wondered why the soles of his little feet
were pink instead of brown, and asked if his blood was
red. They were fascinated and proud to be related to
this new kind of cousin. Our four-year-old niece ran
next door to bring her best friend over to look at Ari, as
if she had found an exotic animal in her own backyard.

While tentative in their approach to our new baby,
Ari's new grandparents, cousins, aunts, and uncles
seemed to delight in his presence. Yes, they could love
him, and yes, he would always be different to them.
They seemed genuinely pleased to witness our happy
ending to a long saga of babyless years that they, too,
had been a part of.

Only once, in Ari's first months, did I hear a remark from a family member that set off my racism radar. "He really responds to music . . . maybe that's the black part of him." We talked about it right away, apologies were expressed, but it took me a while to unbristle. I figured my best hope in combating prejudice—especially the subtle kind that most of my relatives thought they were rid of—was to have them fall in love with Ari.

MOTHERLOVE

Like infatuation without sex.

I stare at this baby, as if looking for his personality. I can't figure out what he likes or what he's like. I'm looking for hints. The more I stare, the more I come to memorize every curve and shape, every ripple and rash. I talk to him the whole time. I tell him that I don't really know how hot the formula should be and that he doesn't need to cry that loud for me to hear him.

There are times when I feel completely inadequate: I don't know for sure how to comfort a baby or even how to hold its floppy head. Would I have known these things instinctively if I had given birth to this rag doll? I should have baby-sat more Saturday nights when I was a teenager. I should have taken parenting classes. Instead, I have to practice on this, my own child.

Whenever he cries, I think I am doing something wrong: I've fixed his diaper too tight; I'm squashing his arm; I've made his bottle too hot. If I can't figure out what might be causing his grief, I jump to conclusions that haunt vulnerable adoptive mothers like me. We fear that our babies are crying because they miss their *real* mothers and know that we are only fakes. At a primal level, infants must know colostrum from powdered milk.

Do other babies cry this much? I wonder if Martie would know how to make him stop.

Someone gives me a book on colic (as if I have time to pour myself a glass of Chablis, draw a warm bubble bath, and ease down for a good read. . . . I'm lucky if I get to shower every other day).

I think I'm bonding, but I don't know if my love could give me the strength to lift a car with my bare hands like some mother once did to save her child (according to *Reader's Digest*, I think). I assure myself it's not normal to adore someone from the moment you meet. Most people need to get to know the person first.

I made the mistake of joining a mothers' group soon after we got home. For two hours each Tuesday morning the women commiserated about their breast infections, nursing schedules, and weight gains; they shared war stories from the delivery battleground. They told me I had lucked out—no labor, no stretch marks —but I knew better.

By adopting, I was not a full-fledged mother in their eyes. I hadn't paid the price of pregnancy, hadn't earned the badge of labor or the award for delivery, and would forever be an outsider—an associate member at best. I looked like the other women, but I felt like less of one.

I was relieved when, three weeks into our supposed "support" group, the conversation moved away from leaky boobs and useless pregnancy clothes. The topic that followed, however, was no more inclusive. Each of the real mothers took an inventory of every resemblance, identifying its origin as if cataloging finds on an anthropological dig. "He's got my nose." "She's got her dad's ears." "That's my chin if I ever saw it."

Then it was my turn. My baby doesn't look anything like me or my husband or anyone I know. He isn't old enough to have picked up any familial idiosyncrasies. Our bodies were never connected as one, we don't resemble each other at all, and mothering does not come as naturally as I thought it would. There is nothing to reinforce the lovely notion that we "belong together." Still, I go to mothers' group, parade the baby around town, smile at him a lot, and cling fiercely to the hope that it will feel like it was meant to be—any day now.

As I hold him closely to me, I stroke his puff of a cheek, his feather hair, his perfect forehead, and tell him that his "Mommy loves him." It's a little awkward to say, but I figure that it's true, no matter which mommy it is.

In the quiet moments—there are just a few—I am struck not by the miracle of birth but by the miracle of adoption. That a legal proceeding can bring complete strangers together, try to meet the needs of all the parties, and ultimately form a family, is really quite profound. The particular match between child and adoptive parent is oftentimes arbitrary, and yet, we don't like to think of love that way.

Nearly three months after Ari came home with us, we were given a date in family court to finalize his adoption. We got dressed up, took the day off, and loaded the camera with film, but what I remember most about the event was the absence of celebration in the busy, somber halls of justice. When our docket number was called (forty-five minutes and one bottle of formula past the assigned appointment), we filed into a hollow, wood-paneled chamber and stood as Judge Marcus Wong sat behind a mahogany desk of armor, asking rote questions about our Social Security

numbers and places of birth. The only question I remember is the last one that he asked: "What kind of
name is 'Ari'? Why did you pick such a . . . such an . . .
unusual name?" Was our competency as parents and the
legality of this adoption proceeding being threatened
by our choice of an ethnic name? I was ready to change
it to "Marcus" if I had to, but coughed up an answer
that was good enough to secure his signature on the
bottom of the document we coveted. Without pausing
for a snapshot or congratulations, we were ushered out.

Adoption is a bittersweet solution to a two-way
problem. Sweet, because a baby in need of a home
finds a home in need of a baby. But bitter because it
is nobody's first choice, and the baby will grow up
one day to understand that.

Ari's birth parents wished he had never been con-
ceived; Martie told us that she would have chosen
abortion, if she had come to terms with her pregnancy
sooner. And Ari's adoptive parents would have pre-
ferred a biological child. Now that he's here, those
facts are hard to admit, but they were once true. I think
about the daughter I wanted less often than I used to,
and more out of curiosity than yearning. With every
passing week and month, my attachment to him grows
stronger than my disappointment about her. I find
myself wishing that Ari had come out of me.

When Ari was somewhere between the ages of nine months and one year, I fell in love with him. I know you're supposed to do it sooner. I had always thought he was cute, smart, even fascinating, but it wasn't until my son had been around for a while that my feelings exploded into the fiercest of passions: the "I'd give my life in a second for this kid" commitment; that "I can't get enough of this little person" attachment; the sheer joy, the complete devotion, the willingness to put his needs first without resentment; the disproportionate pride in his accomplishments; the intimate knowing of another person. I get a little thrill over the fact that he cries when I leave the room. The connection between mother and child is like infatuation without sex. Your world revolves around his; your world would be empty without him.

I think we say we love our children, because we're nervous to say we're "in love" with them.

SPIT-UP IS SPIT-UP

Adopted poop doesn't smell any different.

After an episode—whether it's a bloody nose, a wet bed, a tantrum, or the chicken pox—I think about the question I am sometimes asked: "Where is his *real* mother?" I have all the badges of motherhood—snot on my blouse, Cheerios in the carpet, Handiwipes in my purse, and a car that smells like french fries—but those aren't proof enough.

"If they could see me now," I think to myself as I am mopping up a leaky BM. "Where is his *real* mother?" That vexing phrase goes through my mind in singsong fashion, over and over. "His real mother?" I want to yell back. "She's out getting knocked up by some guy she'll never see again." What could people possibly want to hear as the answer to that question?

I want to tell people that my son was too real for my

son's "real" mother. His "natural" mother did something very unnatural—she relinquished her baby to the care of another woman.

Actually, the woman they keep asking me about is probably working for minimum wage at Marshalls, dating no one special, and dying to move out of her parents' place. Her relationship to this child seems somewhat akin to that of a father who is not home much. Years from now, Ari is not going to love her less for not being the one to wipe his drippy nose.

I don't really expect my eighteen-month-old to appreciate all those dirty diapers I've changed, all those Sunday mornings I didn't sleep in, all those calls I made to preschools. But it would feel nice sometimes to be validated by society as a real mother. "Where is his real mother?" She is right here.

CAN WE RETURN THIS CHILD?

Feelings that top the taboos.

Our two-year-old is acting like a monster. He can't get two Legos to fit together, so he spills the whole bucket and kicks all of the pieces in every direction. "You must feel frustrated," I say, trying to do the damn "right" thing by identifying his emotion. I bring him the juice he has asked for, but it's in a cup instead of one of those juice boxes; he screams in anger and swipes the table violently, so that the carpet gets to absorb one more of his tantrums.

We are leaving the park after warnings of "five more minutes," "two more minutes," "one more time down the slide." Regardless, he slaps me when I pick him up and butts his head against mine in a way that's got to hurt him, too. The worst is when, out of the blue, Ari starts his "taunting Mommy" routine. He raises his hand as if to hit me, laughs if I flinch, and hits if I don't.

There comes a time when a mother doesn't give a shit about the developmental rationale for such behavior and just feels what it's like to be hateful, guilty, confused, and impotent. I can hear it now: "You're his closest love object. . . . He feels safe in letting go with you." Oh, great.

Is this normal, testing-of-boundaries behavior, or is this child somehow aware of being "given up" and feeling understandably angry, hurt, and frightened? I don't know whether to hate him or pity him. If our son is acting out now, what are we in for when he realizes what's really happened to him?

While my two-year-old is acting like a monster, I am feeling like one. I've had hateful thoughts that would get me arrested. I want to smack him, blurt obscenities, leave him alone to make his own damn dinner. I wonder if this whole adoption thing was a massive mistake. I think I've ruined my life. I wonder if I'm trying to make good out of bad genes. I think about returning him. I wonder if my birth child would have thrown that spaghetti at me.

If the thought police were on patrol, I'd be behind bars.

When a bruising afternoon moves past a messy dinner

and into a silly bath time and sweet story before a
peaceful sleep, I leave the extremist thinking of mother-
escape and find myself exhausted. In the calm of night,
it becomes clearer that I don't hate my child or resent
my life so much as I am deeply disappointed. This
isn't the way I imagined it. He isn't who I wished for
and neither am I.

For whatever reason, his behavior sucks. I may not
be able to understand or fix how he behaves, but I
need to be there for him, to stay in the game. I need
to accept our foreverness.

I tiptoe back into his room when the desperation
has let up, and look down on a small, sleeping innocent with his arm around his blanket ball, his mouth
relaxed in an *O*. I want to love him this much in the
middle of the day, when his Power Ranger forces are
in full swing, when his boyness is unleashed, when his
two-year-old body doesn't always cooperate with his
two-year-old brain, when his wounded-child behavior
has a chance to surface if it needs to.

A friend calls to say her kids are driving her insane.
My empty well is filling again. Slowly.

SHOULD WE SEND CUTE OR UGLY PICTURES?

Will she want him back when she sees those dimples?

When Martie chose to relinquish her baby, Ari was an "it" and not a "he," a blob on a sonogram, and not a giggling, brown-eyed beauty. If I could ever understand Martie's decision, it was then, not now. Once she saw him, how did she go through with it? How does she feel knowing that her son is calling some other woman "Mommy"?

When Ari turned nine months old, I remember thinking that he had been outside as long as he had been inside: with me as long as with Martie. Two years later, he's now been with me much longer than with his birth mother, but she is still a presence in his life and mine.

I know her son better than she does, better than anyone does, really. The passage of time has allowed me two gifts: one is to start feeling like Ari's mother, which I do; the other is to stop feeling like Martie might come back for him, which she won't. Open adoption is supposed to quell your anxieties, but it doesn't completely.

Every time we send pictures, we have a choice: Do we send cute or ugly photographs? Should they be close-ups or full-body shots? Perfectly crisp or acceptably fuzzy? Gleefully happy or just contented? Irresistibly adorable or just sweet? A single roll of thirty-six exposures presents us with at least that many choices.

The real question is, if his birth mother sees how beautiful and compelling her son is, will she want him back? The law says she can't have him back, the adoption is finalized. But I think it would be creepy to know that she would if she could. Legal issues and hearts and flowers aside, it's still weird to know that someone could love your child as much as you do.

Our son's adoption was never contested; the records are sealed. I tell those who ask that I trust Ari's birth mother; that she knowingly chose a life for him that cast someone other than herself as his mother; that our relationship with Martie is respectful and important; that our son has a right to know his history. What I don't tell them is that, if Martie or anyone made a move to take him away, I would be a raving maniac, capable of breaking any law, and willing to fight to the death to keep him. Underneath this enthusiastic advocate for open adoption are claws as sharp as knives, just in case.

When I send Martie news and photos, I don't know whether it will hurt her by opening partly-healed wounds, or comfort her by showing that her offspring is growing and thriving. I asked her once, by phone, if she wanted us to continue sending letters and pictures (since we've been the ones doing all the initiating), and she said yes. Period. I still don't really know how Ari's birth mother feels about his adoption; and either she doesn't know, or she doesn't want to say. I wish we could write or call just like friends do, without worrying just how to phrase things. But this relationship is a different kind of friendship . . . if *friendship* is the right word. I'm just not sure how much a part of her past or her present Martie wants to make us. My letters to her every few months have turned into notes once or twice a year, a phone call now and then, and a combination Christmas/birthday gift. Not a word in between from Martie.

Funny, if she asked for a lock of my son's hair or insisted on monthly visits, I'd feel invaded by Martie and resentful of her heightened interest. I'd feel like I was borrowing her car, and she kept checking up on me to make sure I changed the oil every three months and dried it by hand to prevent water spots. I may not own my kid, but I don't want to rent him. At the same time, I'd like to know that she cares. I guess I wish Martie were like a favorite aunt to Ari: interested in his life and happy with her own.

No matter how distant, it's a connection that can't be severed. Martie is forever a part of Ari's life and mine; and he will always be a part of hers. I hope that she'll be there for her son when he comes looking for answers that I can't provide. I hope that she'll lead him one day to his birth father, if that is where Ari wants to go. I need Martie to help me raise our son. I don't need her at bath time, or story time, or bedtime. I don't need her at school plays, or birthdays, or soccer games. But I definitely need her to help me paint a complete picture for Ari, of who he is and where he came from. There are questions only she can answer, commonalities only she can offer.

That is why I keep sending little bits of him to her.

IS IT MOTHER'S DAY
OR MOTHERS' DAY?

No one's serving her breakfast in bed.

My very own forty-three-year-old chef and three-year-old sous chef bring me breakfast in bed: a waffle, a glass of orange juice, and a bowl of strawberry yogurt designed as what is supposed to be my face—two raisin eyes, one grape nose, a slice of apple mouth, and granola hair. Piece by piece, I eat my face, as we giggle in bed until 7:45 A.M.—a veritable sleep-in morning for the parent of an early riser.

I thought about Martie that Mother's Day morning. I wondered if she included herself among the honorees on this holiday. We did. We drank an orange juice toast to both of us, but I doubt that Ari grasped his role as connector between a birth mother and a mommy. To him, we were like heaven and earth: one fuzzy, one clear; both pretty good things, but apparently unrelated.

As the months go by, there are seasonal reminders of our kinship. Ari's birthday is one of those occasions when I feel Martie's presence. I wonder what Martie is doing that day; I doubt that she could have forgotten. I try to call her, which is harder than you'd think, since she moves a lot. What I want her to know is that I will never forget that she is the reason this wonderful child is also my son. But I can't always find her to say so.

One of the things we like to do on birthdays and other holidays is to look at Ari's baby book: an over-stuffed, three-ringed photo album with a white satin ribbon holding together more than three years of memories. He's often too squirmy to sit for long and read with me, but when Ari gets in the mood, we can go for forty-five minutes. That, in the tempo of an ebullient little boy, is forever. On this particular birthday, he sat unsquirming next to me, with one hand pointing to pictures and the other locked onto my thigh.

Ari always opens to page one, where Martie and Mommy stand smiling for Daddy's camera in front of St. Peter's Hospital in California. She is over nine months' pregnant, and impatient. Though Martie's bottom half is cut off in the picture, Ari points a little below the photo album and tells me that he was in there, "in Martie's tummy." It's as hard for me to believe as it must be for him. The story goes, ". . . and then I came to live with Mommy and Daddy, forever and ever." He knows it by heart.

This time, before he said the "forever and ever" part, he asked me where he came out. I wished he meant the name of the hospital, but I knew he meant the body part. He has an illustrated book about the human body that shows the path that a hamburger takes once it gets eaten, going down the esophagus, into the tummy to be digested, and, ultimately, out into the toilet. I hoped Ari wasn't thinking that he had followed the same course.

My mind was racing ahead to figure out answers for what I thought would come next: "If I went home with you, where did Martie go?" "Why wasn't I in *your* tummy?" "Or Daddy's tummy?" "How do you make a baby, anyway?"

Spared. He wanted to move on. Next page, Ari in the newborn nursery, all hooked up to monitors, in a clear bassinet. Next page, Daddy and Mommy trying to feed baby Ari a four-ounce bottle of formula. He wouldn't even take a sip. Ari loves looking at himself and hearing about himself as a baby. No matter how many times I've told him the adoption story, no matter how well he can repeat it to his neighbors and teachers, I know he doesn't get it yet.

Shortly after his third birthday, Ari informed me that he had been born at Castle Hospital, just minutes from our house and, coincidentally, on our way to the park. Clearly, that's where Ari wishes he'd been born; not in a faraway place to another mommy.

I remember one night, in the shower with Ari, he patted my belly and said: "You've got a fat tummy. Is there another baby in there?" *Another* baby? You mean, after all those swell discussions we've had about adoption—the ones where I try really hard to say things just right, so you'll feel safe and special—you still think you came out of me? "Oh, honey," I say to my shower mate, "there's no baby in there; remember, Mommy can't make babies." This time, we move on to shampooing and leave for another time the talk we need to have about the difference between wishes and truths.

I am touched by his desire to rewrite history and am tempted to do the same thing.

There is one character in Ari's story whom I often overlook. James was gone from the scene before I arrived, and my tendency is to forget that Ari came from two people, not one. I have never even seen a picture of the young man whose genetic code is built into my son. I've tried to conjure up his image based on Martie's description—"He's a good guy, he likes sports, he can be really funny and sweet. He's got dark hair, a medium build, long eyelashes . . . he's definitely good looking"—but her adjectives are too generic to be helpful. She has no keepsakes from their five-month relationship except for some memories and his signature on a document releasing him of all rights and responsibilities as the birth father. On it, his handwriting is loopy; it looks young and deliberate. Maybe James is a good guy, but Ari is the second baby he has abandoned into the world in his nineteen years, and I have trouble liking him.

The truth is a gift that I have promised to Ari, and James is part of that truth, like it or not. I speak about my son's progenitor with neutrality, since criticism directed toward James is likely to be inherited by Ari. "He was too young to take care of a baby," I say. "But old enough to make one," I think to myself. For now, Ari doesn't understand the part that James played in his life and he doesn't grasp the losses, but he will, soon enough. Thankfully, kids seem to figure things out no sooner than you are capable of explaining them. And I'm still working on it.

ADOPTION:
THE ULTIMATE BIRTHMARK

Well, that explains everything,
or nothing at all.

Kids do all kinds of weird things. But parents do something even weirder. We insist on knowing where things come from and why they happen. We ardently search for explanations from the past for current behaviors. We seem to need reasons, we thrive on becauses. Many parents hypothesize that Jason picks his nose because he feels insecure, because he needs attention, because he wants to defy the rules. Adoptive parents worry whether Jason picks his nose to comfort himself, to assuage his insecurity about being separated from his first mother. Truth is, Jason may pick his nose because there's something well worth picking in there.

One of the primary filters through which adoptive families interpret the world can be labeled in two parts: "adoption-related" or "something else." It's not that thoughts of adoption stay in the forefront of an adoptive parent's mind, but they are never so far away that they can't be called up in a millisecond. At the slightest hint of an unfamiliar trait, an unaccounted-for quirk, a hard-to-pin-down quality, or an undesirable behavior, comes the question: "Is that adoption, or is that something else?" Like that old commercial: "Is it live, or is it Memorex?"

The answer is not always clear, because adoption issues have a way of sneaking up on you at unlikely times and in unsuspecting places. They are sometimes camouflaged as kiddie idiosyncrasies; sometimes, we'd rather camouflage them that way. We either read too much into things or not enough. From big-deal decisions to trivial minutiae of daily life, adoption looms as a possible explanation for everything . . . or nothing.

Take food, for instance. Most parents of preschoolers don't know how their children subsist. A bite of tuna noodles, a taste of peas, a sip of milk—does not a meal make. Except when it comes to pizza, peanut butter, grapes, and M&M's, food is something you do in between playing. From the kids who don't eat the crust to the kids who eat only the crust, the kids who like nuts in their chocolate chip cookies to the kids who go nuts if they're in there, I expect each of Ari's friends to have an eating quirk.

Ari has a quirk, but it's not one I've seen in any of his friends. He eats frantically. His legs are kicking, his eyes are darting, and food is shoveled into his little mouth as if he's starving. That happens three times a day and at snack time, midmorning and afternoon. He can't be starving, and he knows there's plenty of food. But he acts like he is and there isn't.

Ari's teacher called from preschool to ask me if he gets breakfast at home. She noticed him hoarding cookies, crackers, sandwiches, as if it were his last meal. Just as we do at home, she assured our son that he could have as much as he wanted but need not take more than one at a time. With a full mouth of Fig Newtons, Ari informed his teacher that he was ready for more.

Adoption issue or something else? The something else could be his high energy level or his fast metabolism. The adoption interpretation could be something deeper and more disturbing. Was my son undernourished in utero? Did the separation from his first mother at birth irreversibly wound him, give him an insatiable hunger for security? Whether real or symbolic, how do you teach abundance to someone who's been hungry? How do you teach permanence to someone who's been left?

I assure Ari's teacher: "Of course Ari had breakfast

at home this morning, like he does every morning,"
feeling somewhat like a suspect of Child Protective
Services. Defensive enough to be looking for someone
to blame, I think of Martie. If she didn't want to *be*
pregnant, I'm sure she didn't want to *look* pregnant.
Maybe Martie didn't eat enough; maybe that's why my
kid stuffs food into his mouth. Her womb wasn't safe,
so his world isn't safe.

We'll never really know the cause of Ari's hunger,
but we can try to help him feel psychically nourished.
In the meantime, I have to deal with my own feelings
toward Martie: the feeling that when she screws up, I
get the fallout. I can sense the scales tipping on the
appreciation-resentment continuum which invisibly
links people who need each other. Martie and I needed
each other: She was fertile, I was barren; she had a baby,
I had a home. Adoption was our symbiotic solution.

Martie and I remind each other of the gains and
the losses in each of our lives. The scales are never
fully weighted toward utter love or complete indiffer-
ence: I am eternally grateful to Martie, but wish I had
never needed her. It's a loaded friendship, a complex
connection.

She and I have very little in common, except a son
—and that's no small exception. She is no less related
to me than I am to my son or my husband: all of us

were once strangers; none of us is linked by blood; all of us are forever bound. Martie doesn't get any of the burden of raising a child, but she doesn't get any of the goodies that go with it, either. I think our "deal" is pretty fair, but I may change my mind when or if (and I think it's when) Ari goes through a phase of idolizing his birth mom and resenting his adoptive mom for messing with his life.

I always speak well of Martie. But truthfully, she isn't as impressive as the picture I paint for people who ask. She hasn't come any closer to getting her life on track than when we first met her, at six months' pregnant and without a job or a boyfriend. I thought that Martie would figure out her direction sometime after the baby was born. Now, several years later, she's had one abortion, three boyfriends, several jobs, four addresses, and a brush with the law. She has tried over and over again to restart, and I have believed her each time she's said, "This is it."

Martie seems to have fared less well than her birth son so far, and I find myself uncomfortable with her misfortune. It's true that I care about her, but my wish for her happiness has an added motivation: one that would interpret Martie's well-being as an affirmation that Ari's adoption was the right thing to happen . . . providential, if you will. There's the hope, too, that

Being black and Jewish

Happy Kwanzaa, Happy Chanukah.

When Martie checked "doesn't matter" on the pre-adoption form, she didn't seem to care which religion her child was exposed to. My husband and I were the first two Jews she had ever met, and now her son would be the third.

He was circumcised at eight days' old in an office with bad lighting by a Jewish pediatrician with no bedside manner. The baby started crying as soon as his legs were spread, and I completely lost sight of this as an ancient rite—a *simcha* supposedly, a joyous celebration—that unites Jews throughout the ages and across cultures. We were not surrounded by loving family members and friends, bestowing endless blessings with kisses and coos. There was no kindly *mohel,* no bagels, no *rugelach,* no whitefish, no wine. We will never forget it.

It's our fault, too. Family would have flown in to be there, friends would have come without blinking, but we cocooned ourselves those first weeks, feeling too overwhelmed to be social. That brief interlude allowed us to practice as parents in privacy, while learning about this new roommate of ours.

A year later, surrounded by fifty friends, grandparents from both sides, and three friendly rabbis (comprising a *bet din*, a court of three witnesses), we celebrated our son's conversion to Judaism. Immersion in a *mikvah*, or ritual bath, represents a form of renewal and rebirth; we chose a calm cove in a warm ocean, only minutes from our house. In our arms, Ari was immersed momentarily in the blue water, looking somewhat stunned before smiling to the loving audience that was gathered. There were traditional blessings and homemade poems, happy tears, lots of dancing, and an overabundance of fresh pastries. It was like a wedding for a one-year-old. We called it "Dunk and Donuts," and we will never forget it.

Being black and Jewish, our son is a member of at least two minorities. He knows some Jewish kids and he knows some black kids, but he doesn't know any who are both. The Ethiopian Jews and Sammy Davis Jr. offer little in common with a black Jewish boy living in a middle-class American suburb, though both have been suggested as role models.

Being Jewish means something to my husband and me, but it doesn't mean everything to us. We light candles before Sabbath dinner on Friday night and volunteer on temple committees; we celebrate the holidays with friends and take off from work on the big ones. But being Jewish is not our defining trait. It's harder to teach a child about a religion you take for granted than one that you fanatically uphold.

My favorite temple-going experience does not occur during the special holidays of Rosh Hashanah, Passover, or Purim. It happens during the week of January 15, at a service held in the synagogue to honor Martin Luther King Jr. For one brief hour, members of Trinity Baptist Church and Temple Emanuel sit on uncushioned seats to hear Reverend Miles talk about ten Jews who made a difference and Rabbi Koessel talk about ten blacks who made a difference. They both refer nostalgically to the "Black-Jewish Alliance," when we stood side by side as oppressed peoples during the heyday of the American civil rights movement. On the podium, behind the lecterns, is a bigger-than-life, black-and-white photo of Rabbi Herschel marching next to Dr. Martin Luther King Jr. in 1965, somewhere in the South. For a very short time the worlds of my son—African-American and Jew—come together, and it feels good.

It's not the hard wooden seats that make us uncomfortable, it's the knowledge that current relations between American blacks and Jews are in deep trouble, in spite of this well-meaning, multicultural moment in temple. It's easy to point to the anti-Semitic outbursts of extremists like Nation of Islam leader Louis Farrakhan. Ditto for Khalid Muhammad, the Reverend Al Sharpton, and rap songs by Public Enemy and Ice Cube. But I know that the black-Jewish divide is more mainstream than that, if not as loud. Minister Farrakhan may be exploiting the tension, but he did not create it.

Jews, like many whites, are frightened of young black men. Blacks and Jews find themselves on different sides of many issues, like affirmative action and minority voting districts. Jews as a minority enjoy disproportionate economic success, because they know how to work within the very system that blacks are trying to change. Sometimes, the divide between blacks and whites and blacks and Jews seems hopelessly wide to me.

I'm concerned about the political ramifications of a segregated society, but I'm even more worried about the personal ones. The situation my son was born into gave him no choice but to become a hybrid of ethnicities, cultures, and expectations. Poor kid. We provide unconditional love, a secure home, and as much preparation as we can muster, but he has to deal with the unlikely combination that we've helped to make him.

If we, as a society, are moving toward a world that underscores difference instead of sameness, where will my son fit? Will he be accepted for what he is, or will he have to choose to be only one aspect of his whole? With few models to emulate, I hope my son will find a way to integrate his distinct facets and feel good about who he is in his entirety. I don't know what that integration will look like: Will he wear dreadlocks and a yarmulke? A dashiki and prayer shawl? Will he join Hillel or the Black Student Alliance? Will he get married in a conservative temple, a Baptist church, at City Hall, or not at all?

On October 16, 1995, my son was too young to attend the Million Man March in Washington, D.C., without his parents, who would not have been welcome. In the words of its organizer, Mr. Farrakhan, my African-American son would be a "brother" and my Jewish son a "bloodsucker." Perhaps by the time *two* million black men are ready to march in our nation's capital, men and women of all races and religions will be welcome to join in.

In the meantime, my goals are closer to home. My

home. I want to do all that I can to help my son learn to value himself, and to know enough about his backgrounds to make informed decisions when he gets older. He'll need to sort through the various pieces to create personal clarity for himself and a wholeness that I hope will come.

To help Ari feel good about being a part of the Jewish tradition, we take minuscule steps along a much longer and richer path toward feeling Jewish. It starts with shaping matzo balls for the Passover seder and filling up wine glasses for Sabbath dinner, playing dreidel at a Chanukah party, and dressing in costume for a Purim parade. But I cannot immerse him in a more religious existence than mine, and I certainly can't lure him with bait such as Christmas presents and Easter eggs. Chanukah will never beat Christmas, and Passover will never top Easter, for fun from a kid's point of view. And being different from most everybody else—even if those differences are special—may never feel as good to a child as simply being the same.

FRIENDLY
RACISM

Are they staring, or am I paranoid?

There are a lot of transracial adoptions these days, but people still get nervous when white parents adopt black kids. One of the major objections by the National Association of Black Social Workers and many others is the inherent inadequacy of white adoptive parents to teach their children of color about their children's culture in a way that is not "removed." I agree. I can try to teach Ari about his Mexican-American and African-American heritage, but I cannot be a part of either. His birth parents would provide him that firsthand advantage. Unfortunately, they chose not to. So here we are, white parents of a multi-racial son and, therefore, members of a racially integrated family living in a racially segregated society.

I used to explain that Ari was half Hispanic, a quarter African-American, and a quarter Caucasian. Which he is.

But I came to realize that nobody cares about percentages, and multiculturalism is disconcerting when what people want are labels: singular categories. In spite of his rich ethnic blend, Ari is perceived as black. And we need to help him learn what that means.

Back in our pre-adoption "Dark Ages," I thought race was a nonissue when it came to parenting. In fact, it is *the* issue. We have to deal with race before adoption, because it is more immediately noticeable to other people. I've evolved from an unenlightened white woman who thought all people should be treated equally, to an enlightened one, who knows they are not. And the transformation has sharpened me in ways that scare some of my friends.

When I'm not with my son, people think I'm white. Not a cross-burning skinhead, just a run-of-the-mill white person: enlightened enough to appreciate positive portrayals of blacks on TV and in books, happy to have black neighbors and friends, and unknowingly supremacist, as most whites are.

The assumption of my whiteness bothers me, because I can no longer look at the world with the presumption that things are "right." What I see is the false, white premise upon which standards of goodness and normalcy are based. For me, now, the world is forever askew; something is missing. It has always been missing, but I previously lacked the personal stake that is prerequisite to racial enlightenment. You don't have to search far —from the Candy Land game board, to the roster of teachers at school, or the greeting card section at Pay Less—to see that blacks are either missing, misrepresented, or included as if for extra credit.

In my son's absence, I could be any other white woman, unaware of her unearned privileges. In my absence, he could be any other black male, a source of purse-tightening anxiety that is reflexive in some. What we are together—a very happy, loving family—is not always what others choose to see.

I remember the time Ari found a new friend to play with at the park. The two boys were nearly the same size and equally excited by the cardboard box they had just imagined into a rocket. Sitting on the bench nearby, the other boy's mother opened a bag of Fritos. Faster than the speed of light, the miniature astronauts were kneeling in front of her, hands cupped. "Ask your mommy if it's okay," said the careful lady. Without leaving his strategic post near the Fritos, Ari called to me. I had a Casper-like experience while walking toward the other mom. As if I were vapor, she simply could not see me headed her way. It was only when I got within five feet and Ari beseeched: "Mommy can I *pleeeeze* have some Fritos?" that the other woman noticed me and realized, belatedly, that I was the person she was looking for. "Oh, sorry," she said, instinctively, as if to excuse her preconceptions for blocking her view.

I was invisible at the mall once, when I overheard one teenager ask another if "that little black kid was here alone." Three feet apart, we were unrelated. In a way, my black son is on his own. Regardless of my commitment, notwithstanding my devotion, and despite my love, my son is alone in a way I have never had to be.

To some, I look more like my child's social worker than his mother. We get smiled at and glared at, but always stared at. Adopting interracially is like donning a permanent sandwich board that advertises your adoption (and your infertility, too). Granted, ours doesn't resemble the families on Hallmark cards, but must we explain and re-explain ourselves to strangers—as if it is *our* responsibility to sort out the situation for the confused observer? "Where did he come from?" "Is he yours?" "Did you adopt him?" "Is his father black?" "How did this happen?" I've had to get used to uninvited questions and unwelcome attention, though I sometimes wish that we could be inconspicuous.

Loving my son as I do, I have become an acute barometer of bias: I notice where race makes a difference, and I can't find a place where it doesn't. Attuned to the slightest suggestion of discrimination and prejudice, in even the most innocent and mundane places, my antennae are always up. I've seen racism on playgrounds, in swimming pools, in glances, in books, on applications, and at the doctor's office.

Much of the racism I have seen firsthand is what I'd call "friendly" racism: one of the most virulent strains by virtue of its unwitting perpetrators. I am taken aback that people ask my son if he wants to be an NBA basketball player when he grows up, and ask me if he's from Africa. On his behalf I am offended when complete strangers reach over to touch his curly hair or call him "brother," and I've heard more than one child ask him why he's black.

Were I to challenge any of these friendly people, I'd surely be accused of delusion or, at the very least, overreaction. "Oh, you're just reading into things," or "Don't be so paranoid," or "When did you become such a supersensitive zealot?" Racism, I believe, is never innocuous, no matter how slight or unintentional. It is one thing not to speak about racism but another not to recognize it. The first is unhealthy; the second, malignant.

I seem to have lost my sense of humor in this area of my life.

My son has a beautiful and expressive face: His big round eyes bend slightly at the edges, like upside-down smiles, and his lips pucker like the beginning of a kiss when he is concentrating. Most parents would gloat to hear others say this about their son: "He's a very good looking boy," or "Isn't he handsome?" I couldn't accept the compliment, though, from a woman at the beach who said: "He's beautiful . . . you'd better put sunscreen on him." I didn't think she was warning me about the sun's ultraviolet rays.

When I hear people praise my son's looks I am usually delighted and I always agree. Every so often, my intuition leads me to think that the compliment is actually a code for conveying an indirect message of approval: "We're okay with that interracial stuff." Other times, I'm afraid I am hearing only the first part—"He is good looking" —of an unfinished sentence—"for a black boy."

One afternoon, about the time I pick up my son from preschool, I noticed two African-American girls visiting the school. I had never met them before, and Ari was too busy digging in the sandbox to notice. That's why I was baffled when one of the dads asked me if those were Ari's sisters. "Yes," I wanted to say. "Ari is related to every brown-skinned person you will ever see. They all know each other and they are all exactly alike." Instead, I just said, "No, why do you ask?"

No racism is harmless, but some is downright hostile. One rainy day, our friend Karen took four neighborhood kids to a food court at the mall. Their good time was interrupted by the comment of an elderly man who shouted toward Karen: "Look at that . . . three white kids and a nigger. Look at that nigger." That nigger was Ari, engrossed in his peanut butter and jelly sandwich and spared from understanding such a comment, at least for now. It made us feel sick to hear about it and to know that, much as we would like to, we simply cannot protect Ari from the prejudice and stupidity that exist in our world.

Since my husband and I cannot protect him, we try to prepare him. At the dinner table, sometimes, we practice what to say when people ask Ari about his adoption or about our mixed family. He can answer proudly: "Yep, that's right, I've got a great family." Or with humor, "You mean you just noticed that I don't look like my dad? Took you awhile." "That's right; he has a mustache and I don't."

We talk about the fact that sometimes people are mean to people with brown skin and kids can be nasty about differences. Then we practice standing tall and saying things like: "I like who I am. If you don't, scram." Or, "Go pick on someone your own color." One dinner, we invented a magical kind of armor. It could cover someone's entire body, including the eyes and ears, and would be designed to keep mean words out, and let loving words in.

These deflectors, I've learned, don't always work in the heat of a battle, and I'm afraid my warnings about racism do not carry the stamp of authenticity earned by survivorship. I've been inflicted with human wounds at various points in my privileged life, but none of the insults have been aimed at my flesh.

At a showdown on the playground recently, two boys went from pushing each other, to yelling "butthead" back and forth, to hitting and then kicking: one on the head, the other in the stomach. All this in the few seconds it took for a watchful adult to run across the playground and break the two apart. The first-grader did a better job than the kindergartner at holding in his mounting tears as each described what happened for the after-school teacher. Ten minutes of coaching had them chilled out enough to agree that they would use their words, not their bodies, to work things out next time. But their adult-induced reconciliation might have been premature; as the boys shook hands and walked in opposite directions, one yelled back to the other, "You don't even look like your parents," as if that were the barb that would decide the victor.

Ari waited until he got in the car with me to cry that afternoon. And he didn't stop until nearly dinner. We put Batman Band-Aids on his scrapes, winced at his bruises, and talked about where it really hurt.

WHITES RAISING BLACKS

Good intentions, bad qualifications.

I took my eyes off my son long enough to watch my nephew strike out, which was bad news for the Astros baseball team, second from the bottom in the Little League standings. When I turned back to check on my son playing with a new "best" friend he had picked up on the playground, he was covered in white powder. I saw big brown eyes and a pink mouth smiling at me—reminding me of those awful black jockeys on some lawns where I grew up—his arms and legs white up to his shorts and T-shirt.

Ari was so proud of his evolution into a white Power Ranger, and I could only think of two things: What is that stuff blocking his pores (industrial chalk used to line the baseball field), and was he trying to tell me that he wants to be white? Both were disturbing, though I was less worried about the carcinogens seeping into his bloodstream than about the failure of my efforts to instill black pride into my little powder ranger. It is pathetic to think that a child could wish to change something so unchangeable about himself. Where had I failed?

My parents love me. Love feels good. My parents are white. White is good. If that is the logic inherent in the syllogism that Ari cannot yet articulate, our society does nothing but further reinforce the false premise that whiter, lighter, is better.

Ari notices that he has brown skin; he calls his mommy's skin "pink" and his daddy's skin "yellow." I love that description because it is accurate and non-judgmental. To the rest of the world, however, Ari is "black"; his mommy and daddy are "white."

Ari used to go through black crayons faster than any, until one day, when he told me that black was no longer his favorite color. I feigned nonchalance and asked him what his new favorite color was. "Pink," he said, and my heart sank.

I want Ari to love black, and to have more black things to love. I wish there were black lollipops, black rainbows, black angels, and black flowers. I want to buy videos and toys, T-shirts and birthday decorations without worrying about whether there are only white kids pictured. I want Band-Aids that match him and a pediatrician who can recognize a red ear against dark skin. I want to live in a neighborhood with Sesame Street's diversity.

I am no kufi-wearing militant fueled by black envy. I am simply the mother of a boy who deserves to see people like himself as everyday heroes. The most enlightened adoptive parent knows she can only do so much, go so far for her kid. The responsibility that white parents have to their different-race children is enormous—a lifelong task that we know we can't completely accomplish.

We can read about Langston Hughes and march in the Martin Luther King Jr. parade. We can visit the First Baptist Church for the Kwanza celebration, role play the story of *Amazing Grace,* and talk about prejudice; but it is not enough. It is not enough because it is not the real thing. All we can do as white parents is to love and educate our son; it's really quite imperfect.

We are ultimately inadequate dispensers of racial wisdom; but, even worse, our inadequacy pervades the most basic of daily routines. Take hair, for instance. White hair products and practices do not work on nonwhites, even if the nonwhites are children who can't tell you so. It may be okay to wash my hair in the shower each morning, but it's not okay for my son, whose hair needs washing once a week. He's better off with hair grease than conditioner, and clippers over scissors. African-American skin and hair products don't get a lot of shelf space at our local drugstore.

My life would have been easier if I had had a biological child, or an adopted child who matched. For that matter, my life would have been easier without any kids. With my husband, I signed up voluntarily—albeit naively—for a tougher life. But, as it turns out, it's a much richer one, too. Ari's life, as well, would have been easier in some ways had he been raised by Martie, or by parents of the same racial mixture.

Life is hard enough when you resemble your parents. What have we done by making it harder? What has Martie done by choosing adoptive parents of a different race? I can't figure out if this child should sue us all for negligence or thank us all for ignorance. I love him too much to believe that he'd have been better off with other parents, but I can understand such an unthinkable thought.

MOTHER AND CHILD REUNION

Is she going to kiss him or kidnap him?

My mother gets to me. She knows, from five thousand miles away, the ratio of apple juice to water that should be in my son's drinking cup. She knows that I am late on thank-you notes and sends me Aunt Paulette's address twice. Two times. From five thousand miles, she knows.

She also knows that, from the ages of four to eleven, I ate my daily peanut butter and jelly sandwich jelly side first. We have the same narrow faces, green eyes, long second toes.

Like it or not, I know where I came from. I never thought of that knowledge as a privilege until I realized that my son doesn't have it. That my pinhead matches my mother's is something that I've understood, if not appreciated, over the years. My son has the right to know that he matches someone, too. His fuzzy eyebrows have a reason. So do his talents, and his allergies.

Open adoption provides an opportunity for adopted kids to understand more about their eyebrows, their cartwheels, their penchant for spicy foods, and their A's in math. Every child, every person, has the right to know where she came from and how she came to be.

If Ari's birth mother remained a mystery, she might take on a bigger-than, better-than image than reality would support. I wanted my son to see his birth mother not as a beautiful princess who would let him eat candy all day and then watch ten videos in a row, but as a beautiful person who created a baby she loved but couldn't care for. I need Martie to help me answer Ari's questions in the years ahead, and to help him understand that he was born of a real person, not delivered to us in some mysterious, UPS kind of way.

That's why I knew we should stay in touch with Martie, even though she never initiated the contact. When I called her to say that my husband, Ari, and I would be in L.A. overnight on a layover, she said yes, she'd love to see us.

I wondered if she'd cringe when he called me "Mommy," or smirk when I couldn't get him to listen. When they last saw each other, he was only three days old. Three years later, would he know her? I wondered if he *would* somehow, as if by familial scent, and run into her arms. But Martie was also a stranger to her son, and he had just learned a song from Barney about unfamiliar grown-ups:

> Never talk to strangers,
> That's very good advice;
> You just can't tell
> If they're good or bad,
> Even if they seem nice.
> Even if they seem nice.

Would Ari defy Barney because he knew somehow that this stranger was his flesh and blood? Or would he hide behind my leg and return a smile with an I-don't-know-if-you're-okay-to-smile-at pout?

I wanted Martie to love Ari but not necessarily adore him. I hoped she'd want to hug him but not kiss him on the lips or run her fingers through his hair. What if she seemed to want him back? I had no clue as to whether Martie would be more inclined to kiss him or kidnap him.

Approach-avoidance in full swing, I was jealous of Ari's pre-existing relationship with his first mother, threatened by their right to be close, and secure that I knew my son better than anyone else in the world. I wanted to honor their flesh-and-blood relationship, but not at a cost to our relationship, built from time and love.

Our plane arrived right on time—7:03 P.M.—into LAX. I checked my hair in the window reflection before we got off, just in case Martie had decided to "surprise" us at the gate. When she wasn't there, I relaxed a bit while we went through the ritual of baggage claim, car rental, hotel check-in.

The hotel room smelled stale. Thinking Martie might come at any moment, we decided not to start unpacking or getting Ari ready for bed. We busied ourselves in silence. And we waited. By 9:00 P.M.—an hour after we expected her—we suspected that Martie had changed her mind and wouldn't be coming. I worried that, if she didn't come this time, then next time would be even harder, or might never happen at all.

Concerned, I called her home number. Martie's father answered the phone and told me that she had left two hours earlier for L.A. She should have been here by now. I was relieved to hear that she was on the road but figured she might have turned back after driving partway.

With more disappointment than hope, I stayed in the room while my husband took Ari down to the snack bar to pick up a pizza. When the phone rang, I thought it was my husband asking me to choose between mushrooms and green peppers, but it was Martie. She was down at the front desk! The elevator would be too slow, so I ran down the two flights and almost knocked Martie over with my momentum. She had already spotted Ari, whom she kept staring at while hugging me.

Martie seemed so small . . . even delicate. I had only known her as pregnant. Funny, she seemed much more feminine now than she did three years ago. With her light-olive skin, Martie didn't exactly match Ari, either.

I needed to back away from Martie to get a good look at her. She needed to back away from me to get a good look at her son. She couldn't take her eyes off of him, as he was moving the ashtrays, jumping off stairs, and marching around the hotel lobby. He waved to her from the platform of a bellman's luggage cart.

Martie couldn't get over how big Ari looked. Somehow, the pictures we had sent never indicated that he was tall. She thought he was beautiful (and "smart and hyper," to use her words). "He reminds me of James," she said.

Back in room 211, we shared a large pizza and small talk. Ari showed Martie his favorite truck, a backhoe, and seemed glad for the added attention. We asked about her family, her job, the drive up on the 405. We didn't ask about her heart.

Ari wanted her to read one of his books. Somehow, his old toys and worn books held renewed interest with a new audience. I diverted myself crushing the empty pizza carton as the two were playing, not knowing where to put my body. I was no longer afraid of Martie. Seeing her again, sensing her nervousness, recognizing her bravery, depleted the tension I had magnified with my fears. I wanted to give this mother and son some privacy, but a hotel room offers no hideaways.

Just then, my son asked me to come read with them. Mother-child-mother. I stared down at the Richard Scarry illustrations and saw two brown hands, one light, one dark, and turned the page with my pink version. I could feel Ari rubbing his way into my side, the way he always does when we're reading. My familiarity was an intimate magnet, though I wanted to share him evenly.

I knew that I was Ari's mommy, and I felt a generosity that surprised me. I wanted Martie to experience Ari's messy kisses and hanging hugs. To feel her son on her lap, to tickle him, rock him, hear him say her name.

I never got the sense that Martie wished she were responsible for Ari—at least for quieting him down or for wiping his sticky fingers. She rolled her eyes as if to say, "Does he ever slow down?" I could tell she loved him, though. It was something about how ready her lap was for him, how adoring her looks were toward him.

A roll of film later, it was nearly 11:00 P.M. Our son was losing the battle with his eyelids, and the atmosphere had lost its charge, thankfully. All four of us, sitting on a patterned couch—Mommy, Ari, Martie, Daddy—seemed stunned by the relaxation of such an extraordinary relationship. "If they could see us now," I thought, and smiled privately. Just before Ari slipped into sleep, three parents held their son across their laps, and I repeated something that I wanted Martie to hear: "Before you came to us," I whispered to Ari, "you were a baby inside of Martie's tummy." Without opening his eyes, Ari's little mouth suggested a smile and then went slack.

Martie and I lowered our son into bed, where he slept peacefully. Without the benefit of film, I'll always remember Martie as she knelt down to kiss Ari. She and I hugged for longer than most hugs last. When my husband came back to the room after walking Martie to her car, we could feel her absence.

That palpable feeling of absence is a familiar one for people whose lives have been altered by adoption. It's not as if something you once had is missing—like an arm that's been severed or a dear one who's died. It's rather as if there is something *more* out there that's yours. The life that Ari might have had, the relationship he might have had with Martie—in other words, his subjunctive existence—is not something he has left behind. Who Ari might have been is part of who he is. And the same can be said for me. That I might have been somebody else's mother shapes the mother I am to my son.

It wasn't until after our pictures of the reunion were developed that I could see just how much Ari resembles Martie. The photographs capture striking similarities that seemed less obvious in person: their lips, their creases, the shape of their eyes, and the way they tilt their heads. It's not that Martie and Ari look alike, but they seem to have come from the same place. It is eerie. It is natural.

And so it is from time to time, I'll recognize her face in his.

EPILOGUE

I *go for days at a time without thinking about adoption.*

Ari is five and mighty proud to be in junior kindergarten. He's learning lots of new things at school, some of which excite and inspire him—like dinosaur fossils and writing his whole name—and some of which demoralize and anger him—like being called "dirt ball" by a "friend" and having to go to sleep early on school nights. Life, which is what he's really studying, is often fun and sometimes unfair; it can be pretty complicated and kind of confusing.

At a potluck barbecue recently, he surveyed the hamburgers, cheeseburgers, and hot dogs sizzling on the grill and asked me logically: "Why do we have to be vegetarian?" Vegetarianism is one of many choices that other people have made for Ari. It's one that he can unchoose when he gets older. I fully expect to see my son reveling in a juicy Big Mac, right before my very eyes. It's a viable way to stray from his upbringing, rebel against his parents, and, for once, be a little more like everybody else.

Chowing down a Quarter Pounder is an easy answer to the problem of fitting in. But the other questions Ari has posed in awakening to his differentness—"Why was I adopted and not my friends?" "Why can't we look like a normal family?" "Why am I the only brown kid?" "Why don't we celebrate Christmas like everybody else?"—have no fast-food solutions.

It is with some guilt that I watch my child go through life— in a society that values whiteness and reinforces sameness— and know that I have contributed to making things tough for him. In a world where a kid wants nothing more than to be just like his friends, he is not. Most of his friends are not adopted, many of them are not brown-skinned, few of them are Jewish, and even fewer have families of mixed colors. There are things we can do and have done to mitigate the loneliness of being different, such as moving to a diversified community, participating in adoptive family groups, and working to instill pride and confidence at every turn. But we cannot make Ari our biological child, we cannot recolor ourselves to match, and we cannot turn the world into a place where biology and color don't matter.

It is my hope that families like ours will break through biases with personal friendships, but it is in no way incumbent upon my son to be the poster child for racial tolerance and cultural diversity. Bridging as he does a number of different worlds, he is a symbol of hope for a better future. But much more than a symbol, he, I have learned, is the child I have always dreamed of.

Jana Wolff
P.O. Box 61595 • Honolulu HI 96839
Fax: 808/988-1989 • E-mail: secrets808@aol.com